By Daniel Wallace
Illustrated by Patrick Spaziante
Supergirl based on the characters created by
Jerry Siegel and Joe Shuster.
By special arrangement with the Jerry Siegel family

SCHOLASTIC INC.

All rights reserved. Published by Scholastic Inc., *Publishers since 1920*. SCHOLASTIC and associated logos are trademarks and/or registered trademarks of Scholastic Inc.

The publisher does not have any control over and does not assume any responsibility for author or third-party websites or their content.

This book is a work of fiction. Names, characters, places, and incidents are either the product of the author's imagination or are used fictitiously, and any resemblance to actual persons, living or dead, business establishments, events, or locales is entirely coincidental.

ISBN 978-1-338-02981-9

10 9 8 7 6 5 4 3 2 1   16 17 18 19 20

Printed in the U.S.A.   40
First printing 2016

Book design by Rick DeMonico

CONTENTS

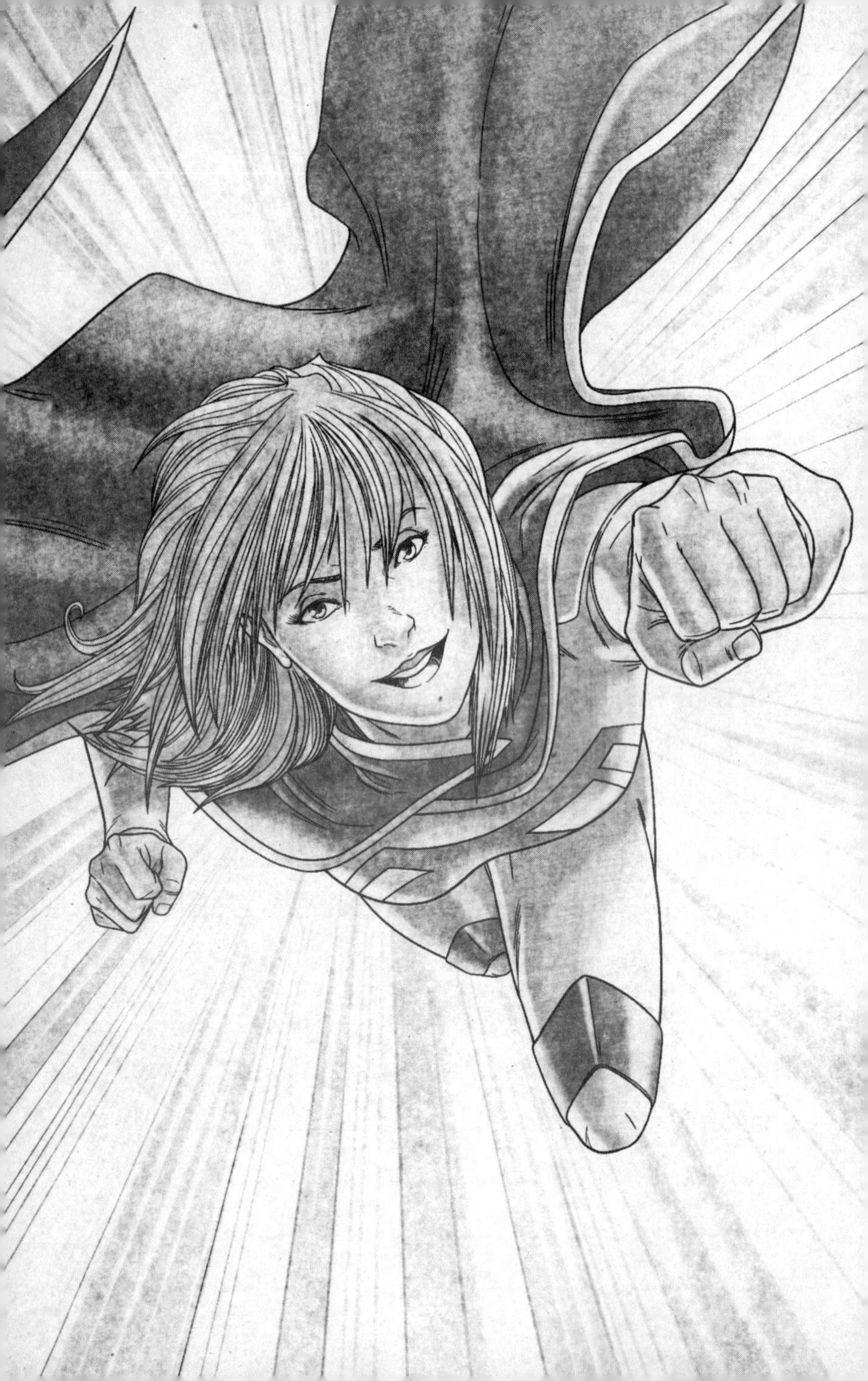

Foreword
by Supergirl

On this planet, they call me Supergirl. Sometimes I still can't believe it—and not just because there are lots of days when I don't exactly feel "super."

You see, I didn't grow up on Earth. I was born on a faraway planet called Krypton. I lived there happily with my family and friends, until everything changed when I was seventeen.

Maybe you've heard of my cousin, Kal-El? He was born on Krypton, too, but he came to Earth as a baby. Kal had an entire lifetime to observe this world's various customs and languages, and to learn how to make friends—or at least, how to keep everyone from freaking out when they discovered that he was different.

I call my cousin by his Kryptonian name, Kal-El, but this world knows him as Superman. When I arrived on Earth, Kal had already become a hero. He wasn't just any hero—he was a *legend*. Right from the start, I had a lot to live up to. It took me a long time before I decided whether or not I wanted to become a hero, too.

You know that symbol Kal and I both wear on our chests? That's the Kryptonian insignia for the House of El. Just try explaining that to everyone on Earth who's already convinced it's a big letter *S*, for *Super*. Unfortunately, being compared to my cousin didn't get any easier once the whole world knew me as Supergirl.

My life wasn't supposed to be like this. Back on Krypton, I was seventeen years old and preparing for the trials of adulthood. Kal-El was just a baby who

I cared for when I visited my aunt and uncle. Then I was forced to leave Krypton, and I spent years in suspended animation before landing on Earth. Now Kal looks older than me, and sometimes acts like it, too. He's had a lot more experience using his powers, and he perfectly fulfills the role of beloved Super Hero. I had to figure out where I would fit in to this new planet.

But I'm not sorry. I am the last daughter of another world. Every time I feel like I don't belong on Earth, I remember that I carry within me the history of my people and the traditions of my home world. From my parents, Zor-El and Alura, I learned the value of scientific thinking and the importance of never giving up. I am proud to carry on the legacy of Krypton, and to incorporate my heritage with all the new experiences I've had on Earth.

I am Kara Zor-El: daughter of Zor-El and Alura, cousin of Kal-El, and the last to carry memories of the real Krypton. I am Supergirl.

Friends, Foes, and Family

Zor-El

Supergirl's father on the planet Krypton. He tried to save his home, Argo City, from Krypton's destruction, but in the end he could save only his daughter.

Alura

Supergirl's mother on the planet Krypton. She taught her daughter to think before acting and helped her prepare for the trials of adulthood.

Superman

Also known by his Kryptonian name, Kal-El, Superman is Supergirl's cousin. He arrived on Earth before Supergirl did and got a head start in adapting to the customs of this strange new place.

Simon Tycho

A billionaire inventor who believes that the secrets of alien technology will make him even more rich and powerful. After Supergirl arrived on Earth, she became his target.

Siobhan Smythe

A young woman from Ireland, and Supergirl's roommate. She is also known as the Silver Banshee and has sonic-scream powers.

Power Girl

In the parallel dimension of Earth 2, a different Kara Zor-El grew up to become Power Girl. After leaving Earth 2, Power Girl became Supergirl's friend.

Dr. Shay Veritas

A brilliant Earth scientist, Dr. Veritas originally helped Superman understand his powers. She later became an ally of Supergirl's as well.

Reign

A powerful warrior created by the Kryptonian military to serve as a living weapon. As the leader of the Worldkillers, she tried to take over Earth.

Chronology

Kara Zor-El grows up in Argo City on Krypton. When she reaches the age of seventeen, she begins her training for the trials of adulthood.

Kara's father, the scientist Zor-El, discovers that the planet Krypton is going to explode and that nothing he can do will stop it. In secret, he makes preparations.

Superman finds Kara. He explains that he is her cousin, Kal-El, and that he grew up on Earth while she remained in suspended animation.

The rocket that brought Kara to Earth is stolen by billionaire Simon Tycho. He sets up experiments to test Kara's superpowers, but she escapes.

Not believing Superman's story that Krypton is gone forever, Kara travels back home to see for herself.

At the bottom of the Atlantic Ocean, Supergirl builds a secret base that she calls the Sanctuary of Solitude.

Supergirl meets her counterpart from another universe, a woman who calls herself Power Girl. The two become close friends.

Supergirl joins other Super Heroes of Earth as a member of the Justice League.

Zor-El realizes that he can save only one person from Krypton's destruction. He places his daughter Kara in suspended animation and sends her in a rocket toward Earth.

Kara's rocket spends many years orbiting Earth's yellow sun. While Kara remains safely asleep, the sun's rays energize her superpowers.

The rocket finally lands on Earth. When Kara wakes up, she doesn't remember what happened to her and is confused and frightened by her unexpected superpowers.

In the ruins of Argo City, Kara meets a super-powered woman named Reign and follows her back to Earth to prevent her from conquering the planet.

Kara defeats the Worldkillers in downtown New York City. With this victory, she becomes the world's newest Super Hero: Supergirl!

Supergirl makes a new life for herself on Earth. She finds a roommate, Siobhan Smythe, and gets a job to help her understand her new home's strange customs.

The Cyborg Superman and other enemies threaten Supergirl, but she defeats them and stands ready to defend the world from future menaces.

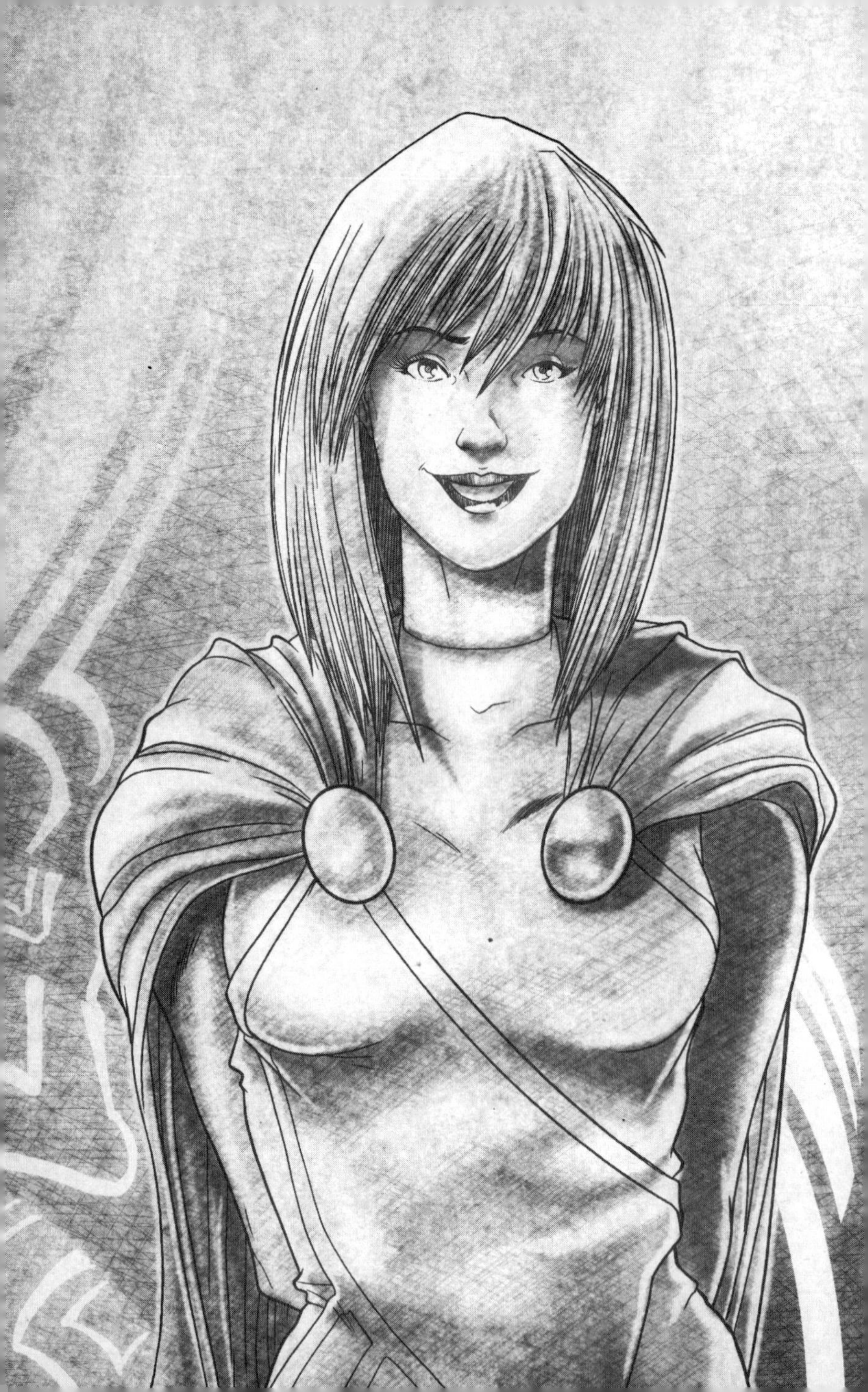

CHAPTER ONE

THE WORLD OF KRYPTON

Kara Zor-El liked traveling and spending time with her friends. She loved her parents but sometimes fought with them, too. And she had big dreams for her future. She was like many seventeen-year-olds all over the universe, but with one big difference—Kara Zor-El lived on the planet Krypton.

The people of Krypton looked like the people of Earth, but the world they inhabited wasn't one that any human being would recognize. Krypton had perfected advanced technology centuries ago. The Ruling Council decided that because their people had everything they needed, it was better to keep everything the same and maintain their success, rather than attempt to push their technologies further and risk failure. To keep life on Krypton safe and predictable, extended family networks—or Houses—all performed the same jobs. Kara belonged to the House of El, which was made up of scientists.

Zor-El and Alura, Kara's parents, were scientists, as were her aunt and uncle. Every time Kara visited Kryptonopolis to see Uncle Jor-El and Aunt Lara, she spent time caring for their baby boy, Kal-El. One day, her baby cousin would follow the same career path as his parents. After Kara reached her eighteenth birthday and passed the trials of adulthood, she would become a scientist, too.

That was the way of life on Krypton: Everyone knew their role and what was expected of them. No one ever woke up wondering what would happen.

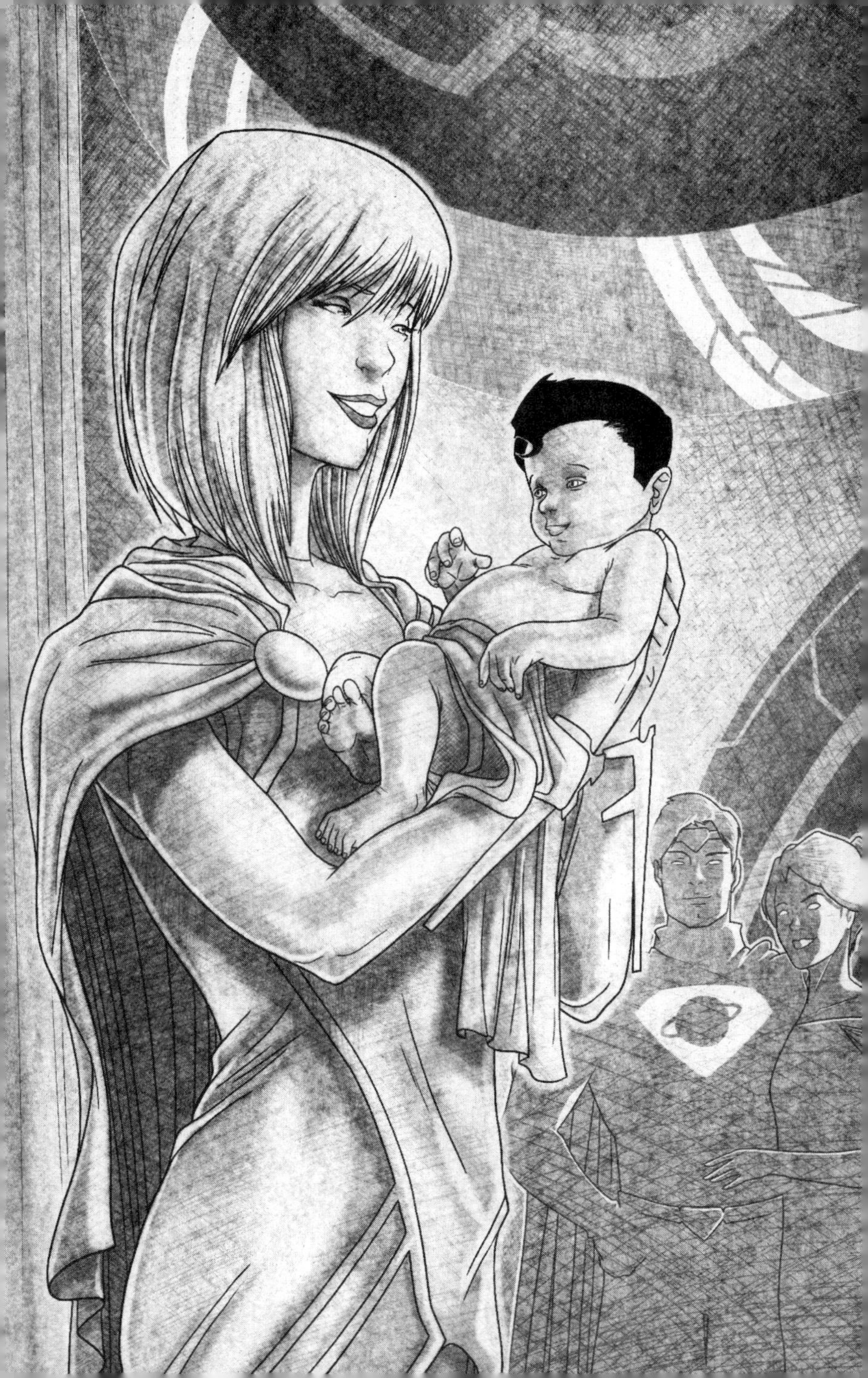

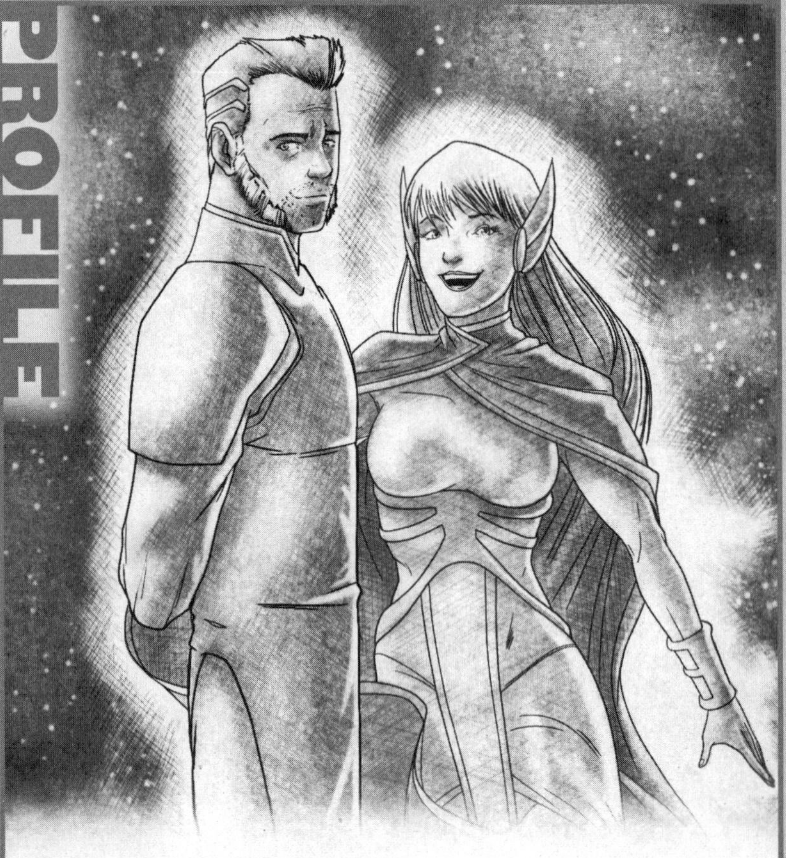
PROFILE

Zor-El and Alura

Supergirl's parents, Zor-El and Alura, were leading members of Krypton's scientific class. Zor-El learned that Krypton would soon explode, but failed to convince the planet's leaders of the danger. In a laboratory in the family's hometown of Argo City, Zor-El built a spacecraft to transport his daughter, Kara Zor-El, to safety, allowing her to start a new life on the planet Earth. Her parents' sacrifice continues to inspire Supergirl to achieve great things.

Kara's family, however, had a history of pushing boundaries. Her father, Zor-El, had a flair for experimentation, and many of the devices he had invented in Kara's hometown of Argo City angered the rulers of Krypton. The planet's military caste violently punished scientists and other free thinkers under the orders of General Zod. None of that seemed to scare Kara's father, who had just finished building a ring of power generators around Argo City. If they worked according to plan, they would supply the city's residents with unlimited energy.

Kara looked down at Argo City from the window of a public air car. As familiar as the sights were, she always enjoyed how different they looked when she saw them from a new perspective. The air car passed beneath the Argo Lightbridge, with Krypton's red sun glowing overhead and the golden shimmer of the firefalls far below. After passing around the Hope Spire, the transport touched down on the green expanse leading to the Infinity Gardens.

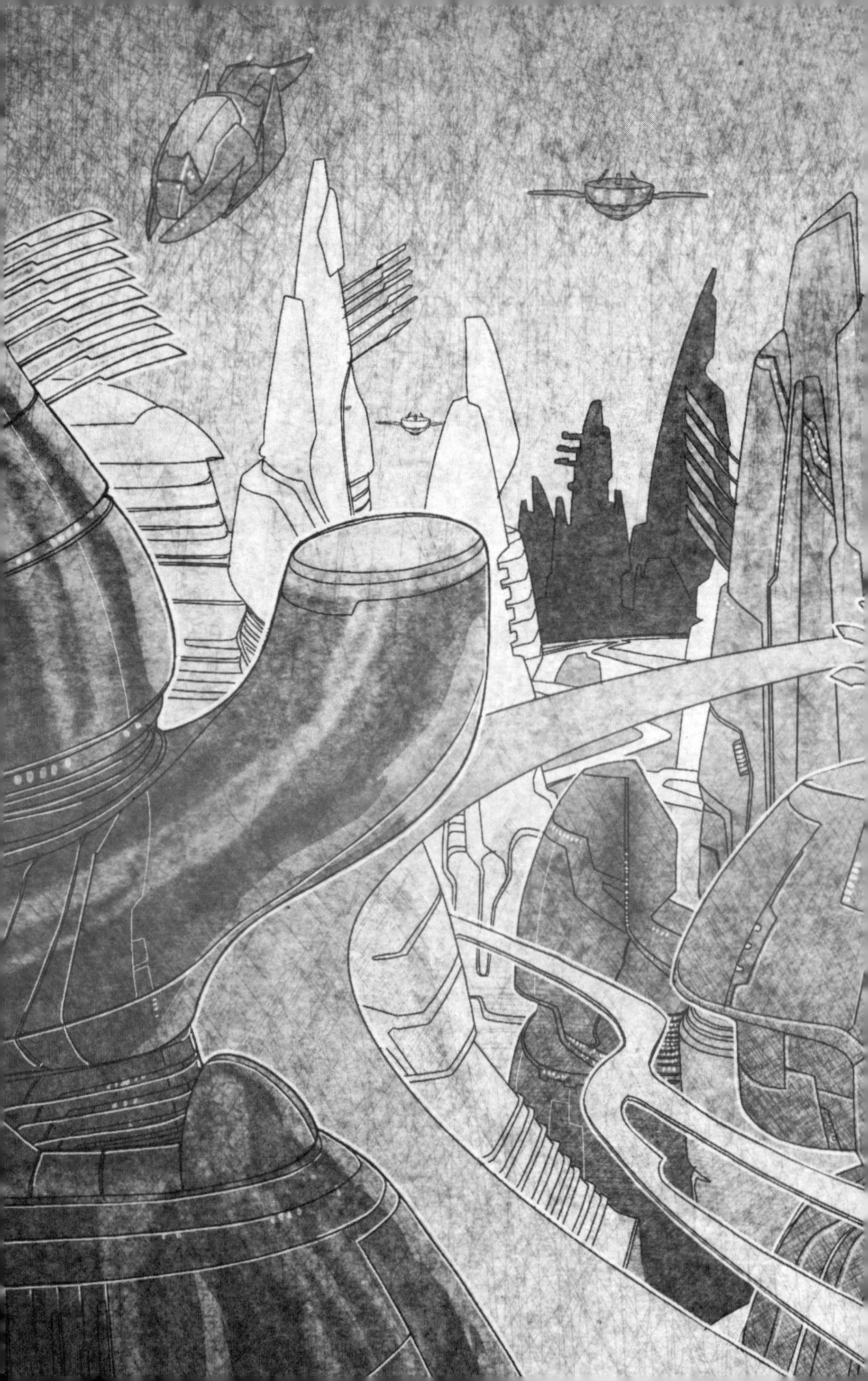

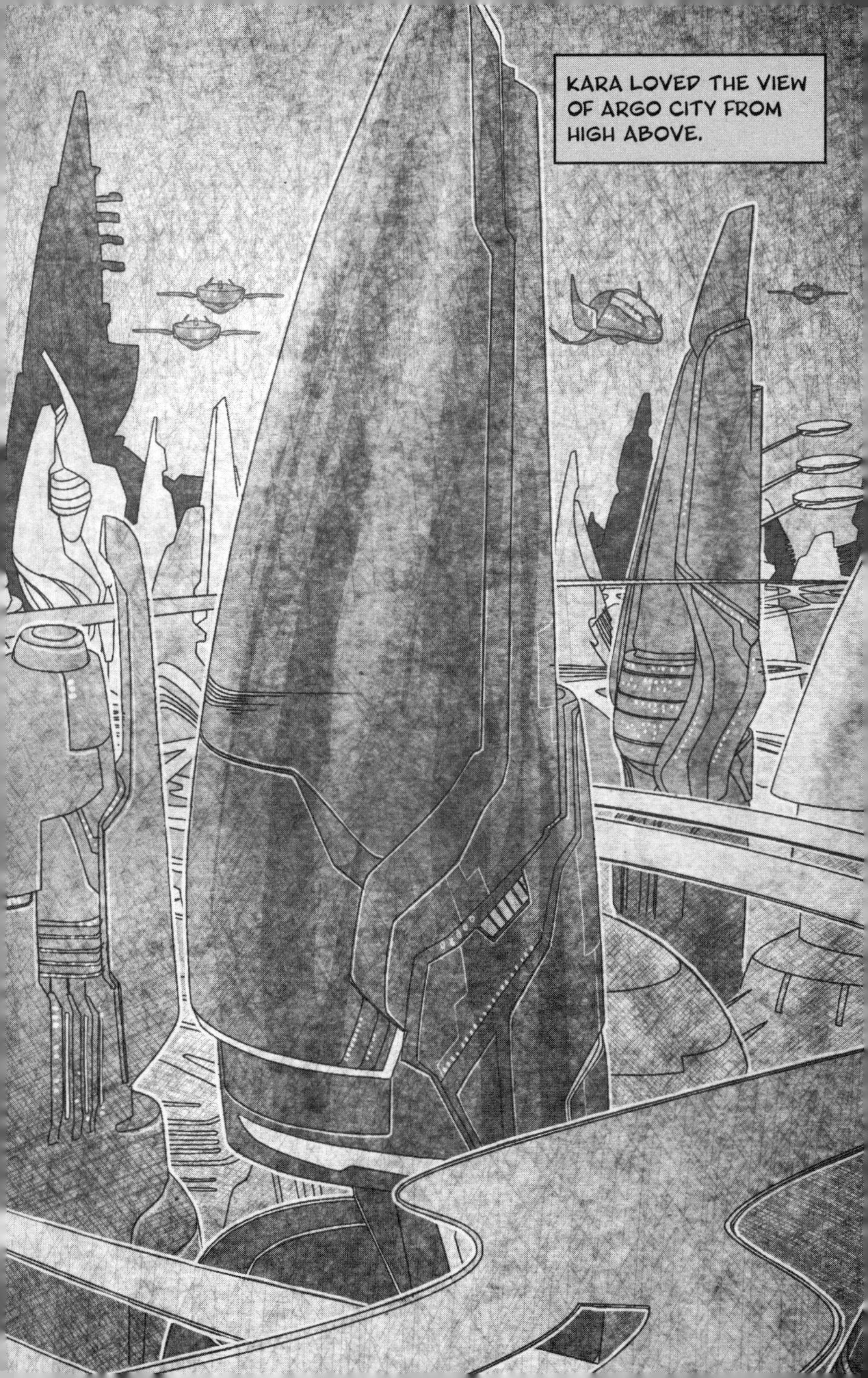
KARA LOVED THE VIEW OF ARGO CITY FROM HIGH ABOVE.

Kara disembarked and raced home. She was late for her sparring session.

The trials of adulthood were a big step on Krypton. Teenagers needed to prove their fitness in

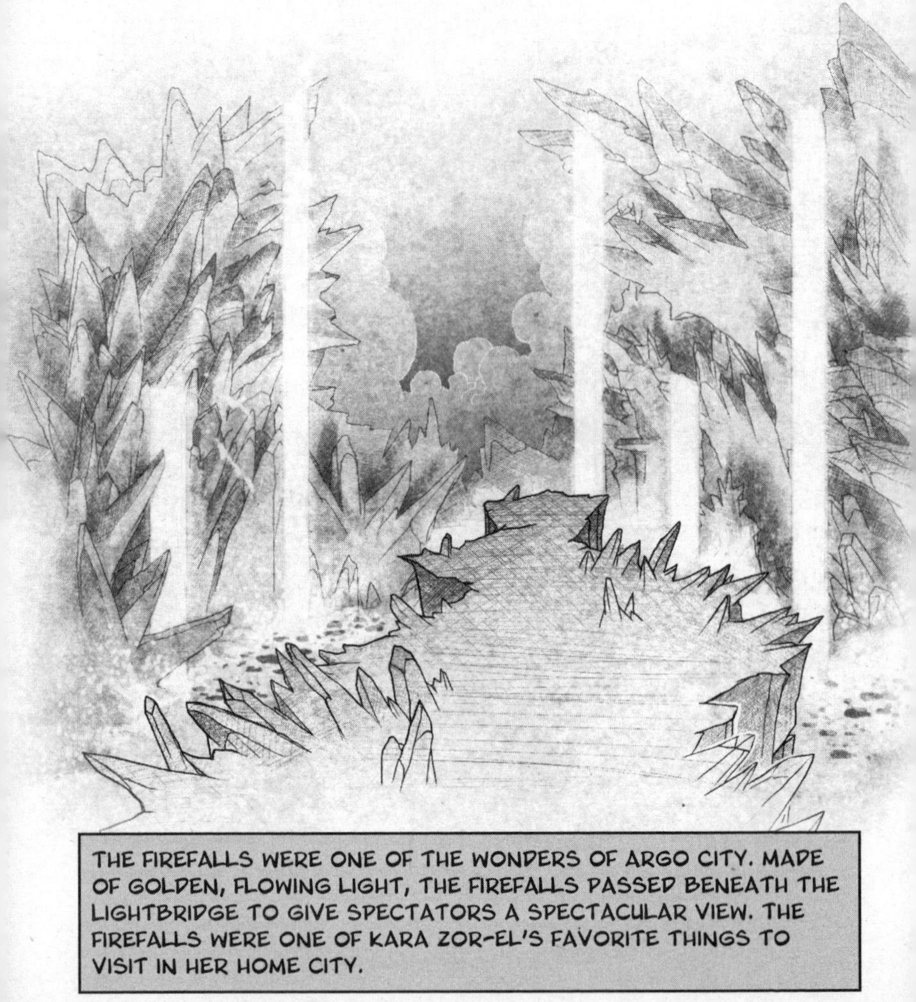

THE FIREFALLS WERE ONE OF THE WONDERS OF ARGO CITY. MADE OF GOLDEN, FLOWING LIGHT, THE FIREFALLS PASSED BENEATH THE LIGHTBRIDGE TO GIVE SPECTATORS A SPECTACULAR VIEW. THE FIREFALLS WERE ONE OF KARA ZOR-EL'S FAVORITE THINGS TO VISIT IN HER HOME CITY.

both mind and body before earning full citizenship. Kara changed into loose-fitting clothes and squared off against the training robot, which activated its holographic shields for absorbing Kara's strikes and kicks. As the two traded blows, Kara caught a glimpse of her father in the doorway. Zor-El had a low opinion of combat, believing that brainpower was the only thing a scientist needed. Kara wiped her forehead and shot him a smile. She was having too much fun stretching her muscles to worry about what her father thought.

The sparring robot's arm jabbed forward. Anticipating the punch, Kara ducked and swept her leg, knocking her opponent to the floor. She stood up, breathing heavily.

As soon as she passed the trials, Kara would be allowed to wear the crest of the House of El and be recognized as a citizen by the elders of Krypton. Because she had no brothers or sisters—and because and Kal-El was only a baby—Kara would be the

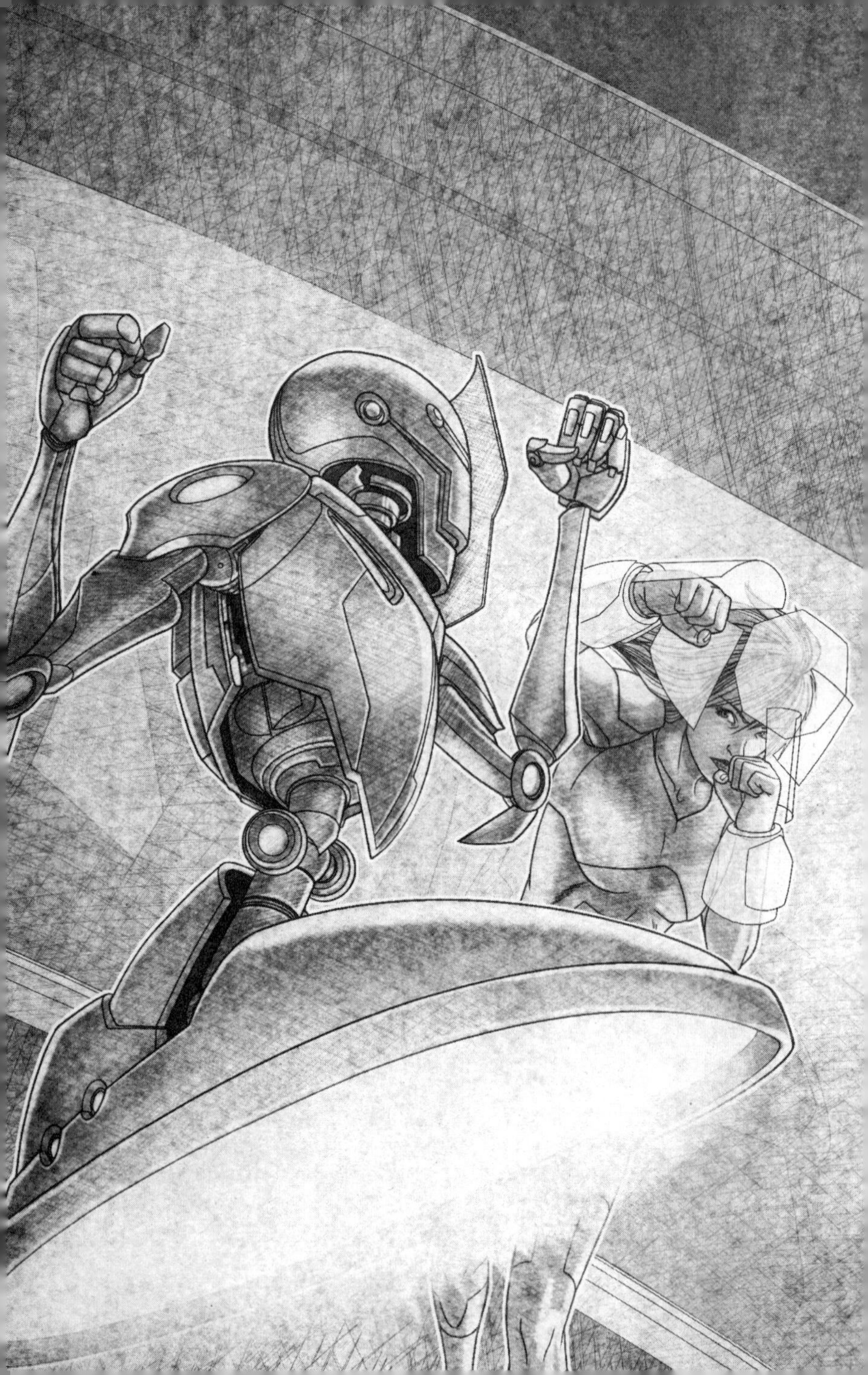

first member of the House of El to pass the trials in years. She knew what the future held, and the thought made her feel confident and secure.

Kara cleaned up and changed into fresh clothes. She still had time to catch up on crystalline sunstone data encoding before taking a break for dinner. The trials would be here before she knew it, and she wasn't going to go in unprepared.

Kara sat down and activated her desktop hologram. A light beeped urgently at the corner of the display. It was a message from her father, who said he had important news to share.

Kara couldn't shake the feeling that this was news she wouldn't like.

DURING HER TRAINING, KARA ZOR-EL SIGNED UP FOR DAILY SPARRING SESSIONS WITH A COMBAT ROBOT. THE ROBOT HOVERS ABOVE THE GROUND USING AN ANTIGRAVITY FIELD AND IS PROGRAMMED NOT TO INJURE ITS OPPONENTS.

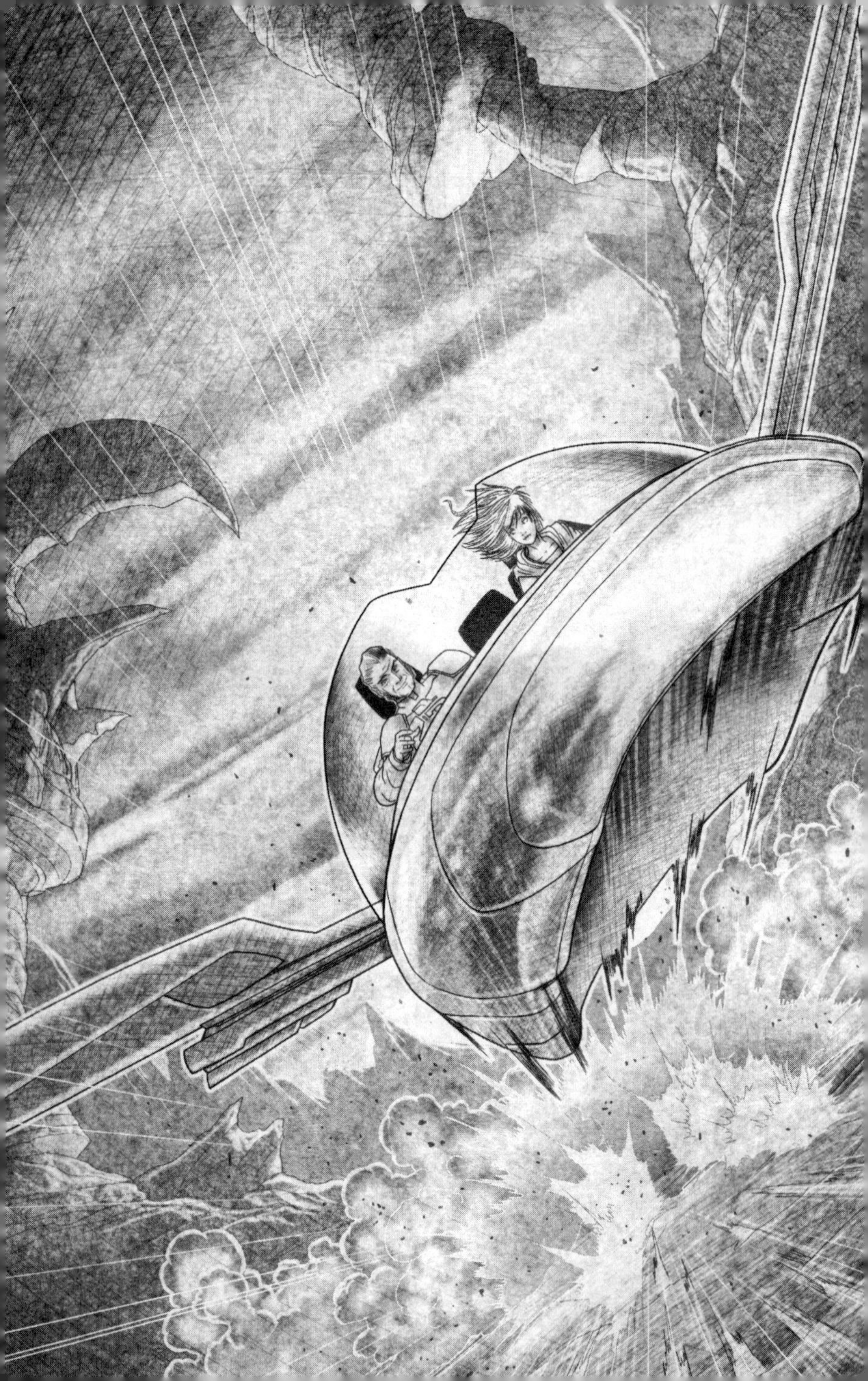

CHAPTER TWO

DESTRUCTION

Kara poked her head through the doorway of their home's exterior courtyard. Her father was there, tinkering with the engine of a two-person air car. This air car model had been manufactured in the millions all across Krypton, but her father couldn't resist modifying his own car with a few extra tricks. Just because this one *looked* like everyone else's, Zor-El said, didn't mean it wasn't special.

Today, Zor-El didn't have his usual sharp-eyed

enthusiasm. Nodding heavily to his daughter, he climbed behind the controls of the air car as Kara slipped into the passenger seat. Rising above the ground, the car turned away from the spectacular downtown of Argo City toward its barren, rocky outskirts. Kara wondered if they were heading toward his father's new power generators, but instead Zor-El dropped the craft into a narrow canyon. After slipping into the dark shadow between two boulders, the air car touched down inside Zor-El's secret lab.

Kara had been here many times. Once, she had asked her father why he hadn't built his lab closer to the noises and crowds of Argo City. He had answered honestly, telling his daughter that he didn't always trust everyone in Krypton. Krypton's Ruling Council and its military caste had power, and Zor-El believed that they did not use their power wisely.

The darkened laboratory was still familiar, but today everything seemed tinged by a sadness Kara found difficult to explain. On a raised platform in the central chamber sat a machine Kara had never seen before. It looked a little bit like a small air car, but with larger, more powerful engines and without any windows.

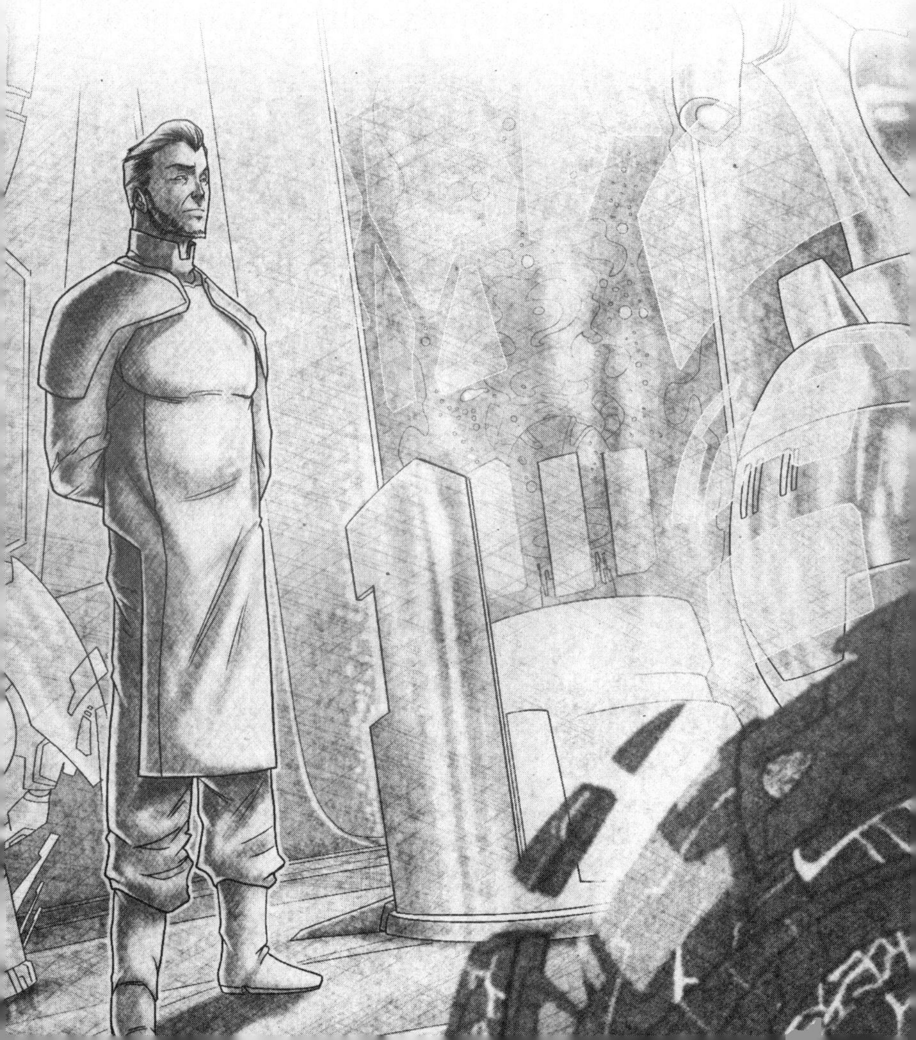

It was what lay on top of the craft that caught Kara's eye. She took a sharp breath as she recognized the neatly folded rectangle of blue, red, and yellow. Her father smiled, waving her forward. Kara grabbed the material and held it high, watching as it unfolded to its full length.

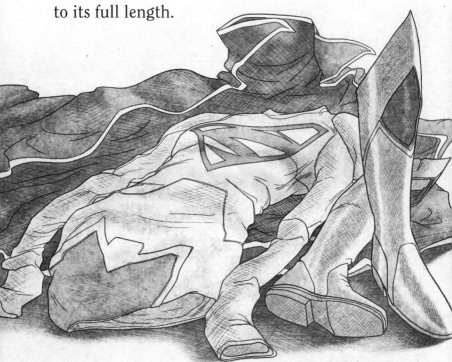

ADULT KRYPTONIANS WEAR SUITS SIMILAR TO THIS ONE AS A SIGN THAT THEY HAVE PASSED THE TRIALS OF ADULTHOOD. THE ENTIRE COSTUME, INCLUDING THE BOOTS AND THE CAPE, ARE MADE FROM AN ADVANCED MATERIAL THAT IS ALMOST IMPOSSIBLE TO RIP, BURN, OR OTHERWISE DESTROY.

It was her House of El uniform. She wasn't supposed to wear it yet, not until she passed the trials of adulthood, but her father looked so proud to see her holding it. Kara ran her fingers across the fabric. A product of Kryptonian technology, the clothing was light and flexible, yet stronger than a suit of armor. With a wash of relief, Kara realized that this early gift must be the reason for her father's strange behavior. She had been worried over nothing.

Kara ducked into a side room to try it all on, and emerged decked from head-to-toe in Kryptonian ceremonial wear. High boots and a long cape added touches of formal elegance to an outfit that carried the weight of thousands of years of her family's heritage. The triangular shape on her chest contained a symbol curved back on itself like a serpent, announcing her status as a member of the House of El. Her heart soared with pride.

When she looked at her father, however, Kara knew that something wasn't right. Zor-El wasted no time. "Krypton is doomed," he began, his voice barely above a whisper. Kara had never known her father to lie. And when it came to matters of science, she had never known him to make a mistake.

The words seemed to come to him easier now, and Zor-El explained it all: The truth behind the ground quakes that had recently shaken Krypton and the origin of the green radiation that was poisoning the planet's core. How he had tried, and failed, to convince the Ruling Council to take action to reverse the damage to the planet. Only one person—his brother, Jor-El—had supported his claims. No one else wanted to hear the horrifying truth.

Krypton would explode; it was only a matter of when. But there was still one last shred of hope. Though the power generators Zor-El had installed around Argo City would no longer supply energy for future generations, they could be used to generate a force field around the city. The city might survive the explosion—but it was a million-to-one shot. And

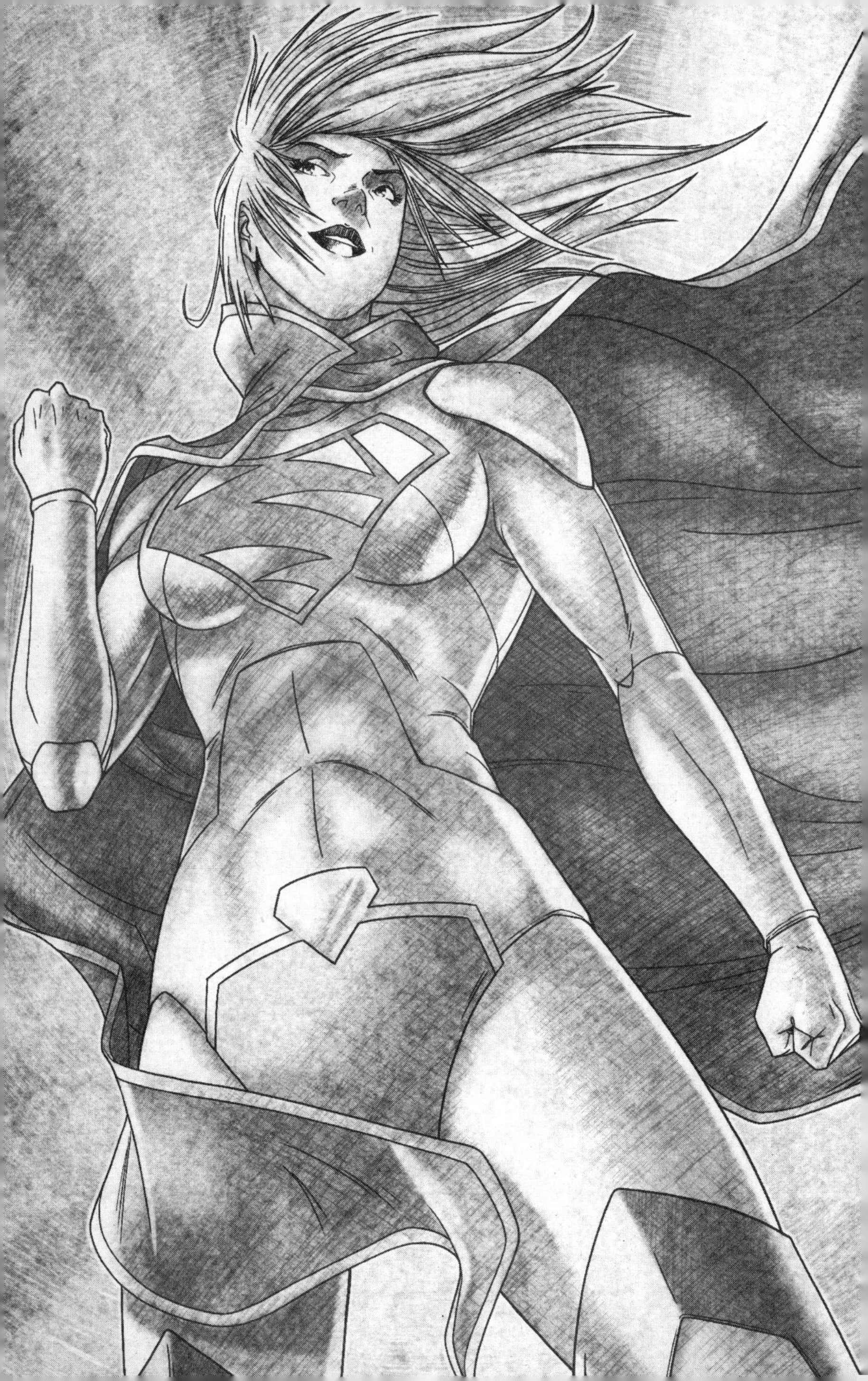

Zor-El loved his daughter too much to risk her fate to those odds.

The small craft Kara had seen in the lab was an interstellar rocket designed to carry a single person to safety. It would bring Kara to a distant planet and orbit a yellow star for years while she remained in suspended animation, never aging until she emerged. The solar radiation would make her strong in ways she could never imagine. She would have a new life, even if Zor-El and Alura would not be around to see it.

Kara felt sick. It was too much to take in. Her future in the House of El, moments ago so close to her reach, would never happen. This catastrophe would bring about the end of everyone she had ever known and loved.

Kara immediately refused to go. She wouldn't abandon her family. She would stay and help. She took a step forward, but her knee buckled and she crumpled to the floor. Everything went dark.

Zor-El stepped away from the machine that had put his daughter into suspended animation. He confirmed that she had slipped into a deep sleep. It broke his heart, but this was the only way Kara could survive.

He placed his daughter inside the rocket and activated its controls. The metallic craft shot from the lab, soaring one last time above the wonders of

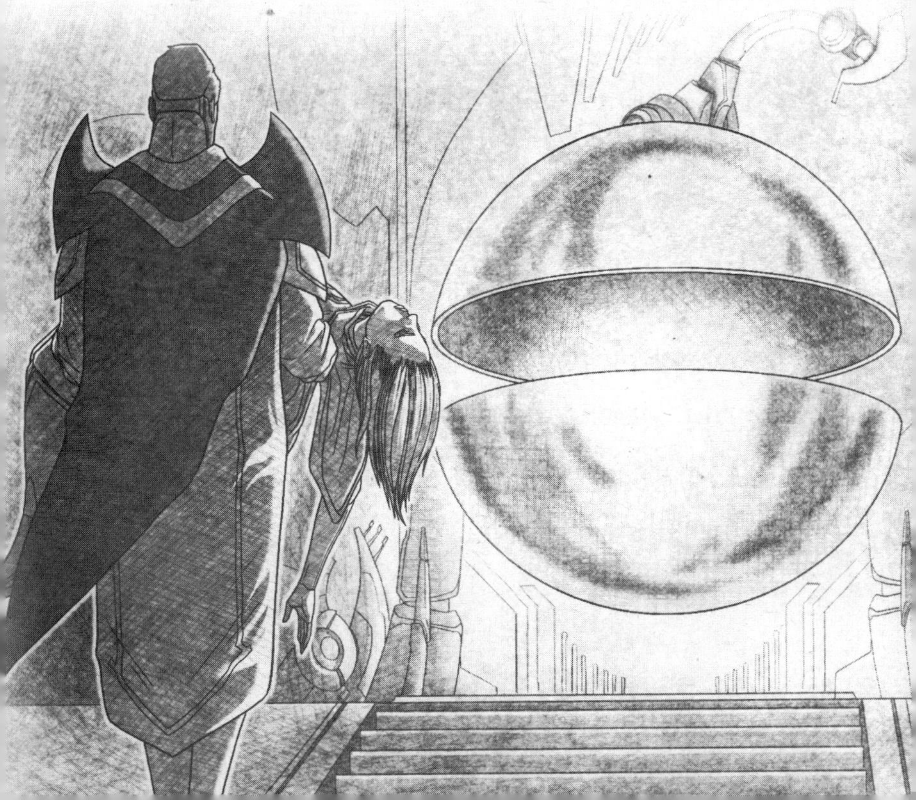

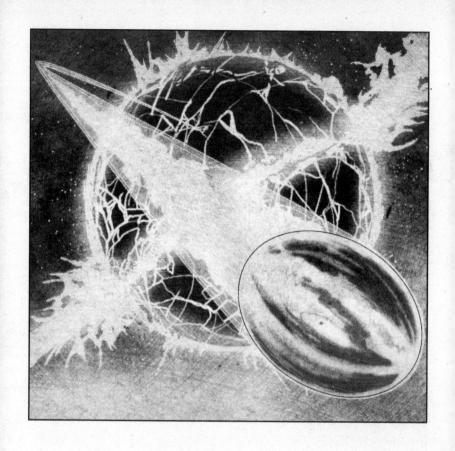

Argo City. A moment later it roared through the planetary atmosphere.

Zor-El watched the fading streak left by the rocket's path as a violent tremor shook the floor. Krypton's destruction had begun.

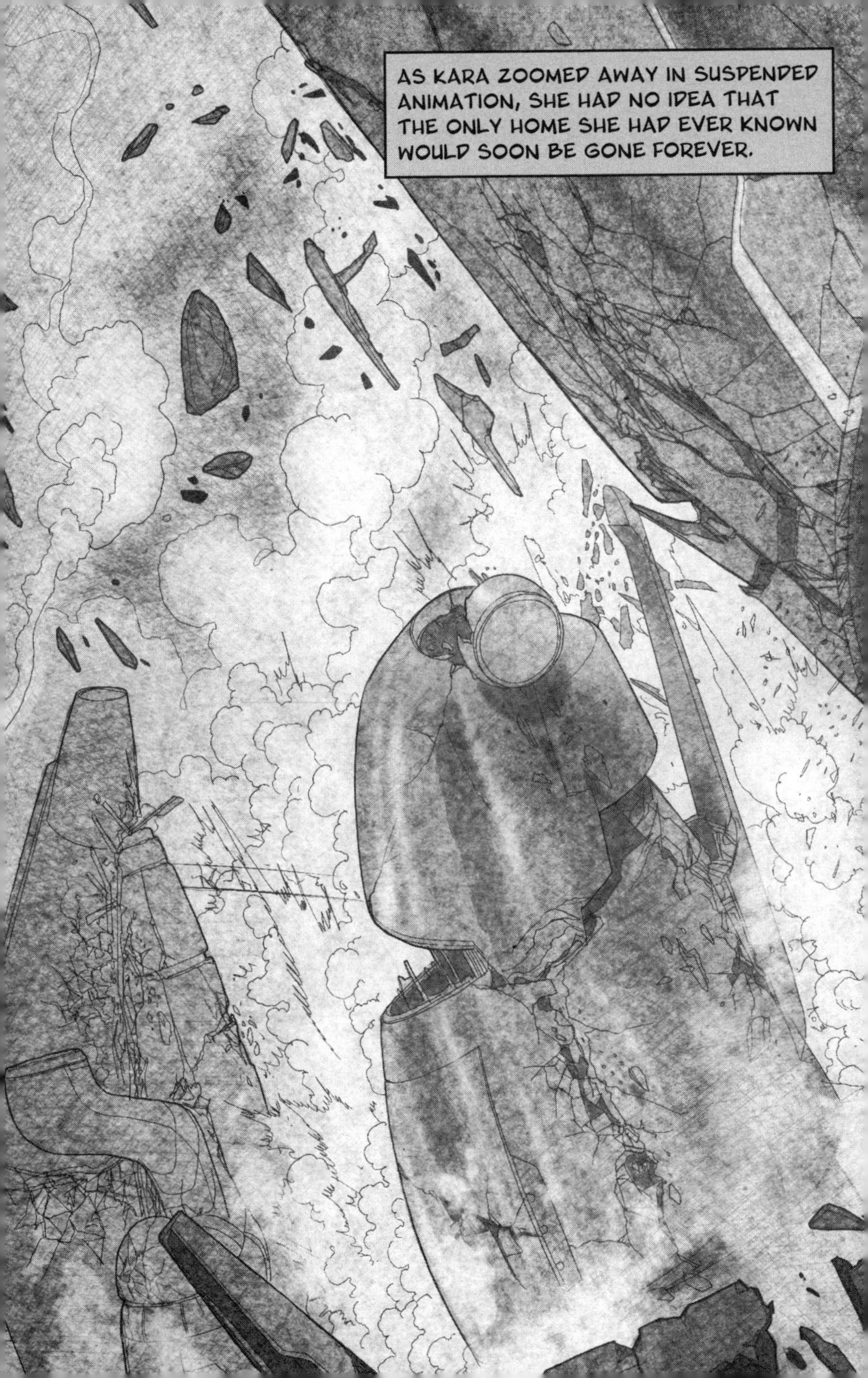
AS KARA ZOOMED AWAY IN SUSPENDED ANIMATION, SHE HAD NO IDEA THAT THE ONLY HOME SHE HAD EVER KNOWN WOULD SOON BE GONE FOREVER.

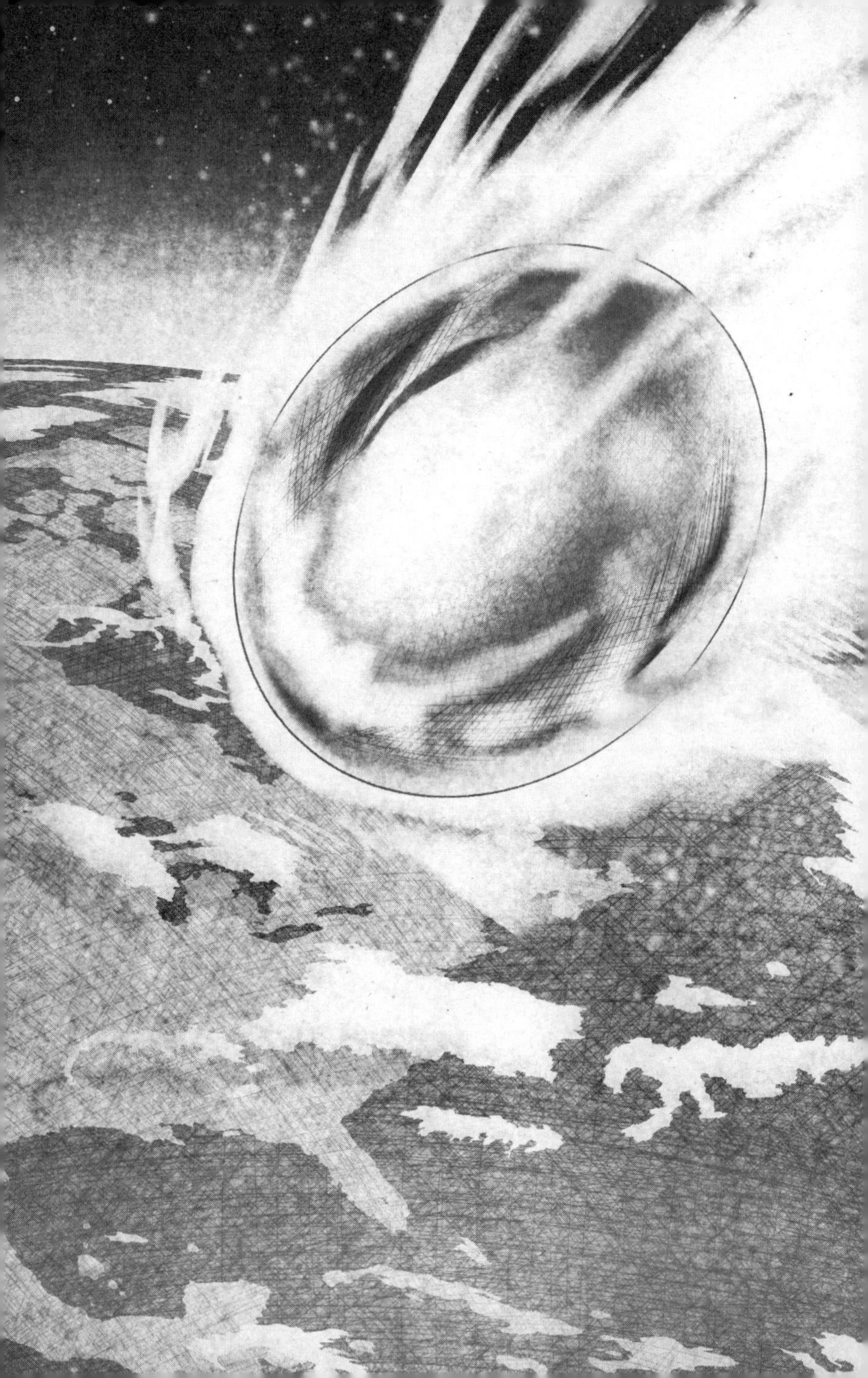

CHAPTER THREE

ARRIVAL

A long time passed as Kara's rocket crossed the stars. The craft spent an even longer period circling the yellow sun at the center of its chosen planetary system. The healthy rays penetrated the ship's metal hull and energized its sleeping passenger.

When the rocket finally whirred back to life, it fired its engines in the direction of a nearby blue-and-green world—a planet known to its inhabitants as Earth.

39

Kara's rocket burned though the Earth's atmosphere, losing pieces of its outer shell as it plummeted. It slammed into the ground in a remote area on the planet's largest landmass: an expanse of frozen tundra called Siberia. At the bottom of the crater it had made, the spacecraft hissed as its metal skin cooled. A seam on its upper surface widened and a hatch swung open. Kara Zor-El stood up on unsteady legs, hugging her shoulders in the chilly air.

She wasn't alone. At least half a dozen strange figures surrounded the pod in every direction. All of them wore heavy armor that made them look twice their size.

Kara took in the scene and struggled to remember what had happened. Her long sleep had disoriented her, and she shook her head in an unsuccessful attempt to clear her foggy brain. On Krypton, only the soldier caste wore armor of this type. If these were soldiers, had they been sent here to investigate the crash?

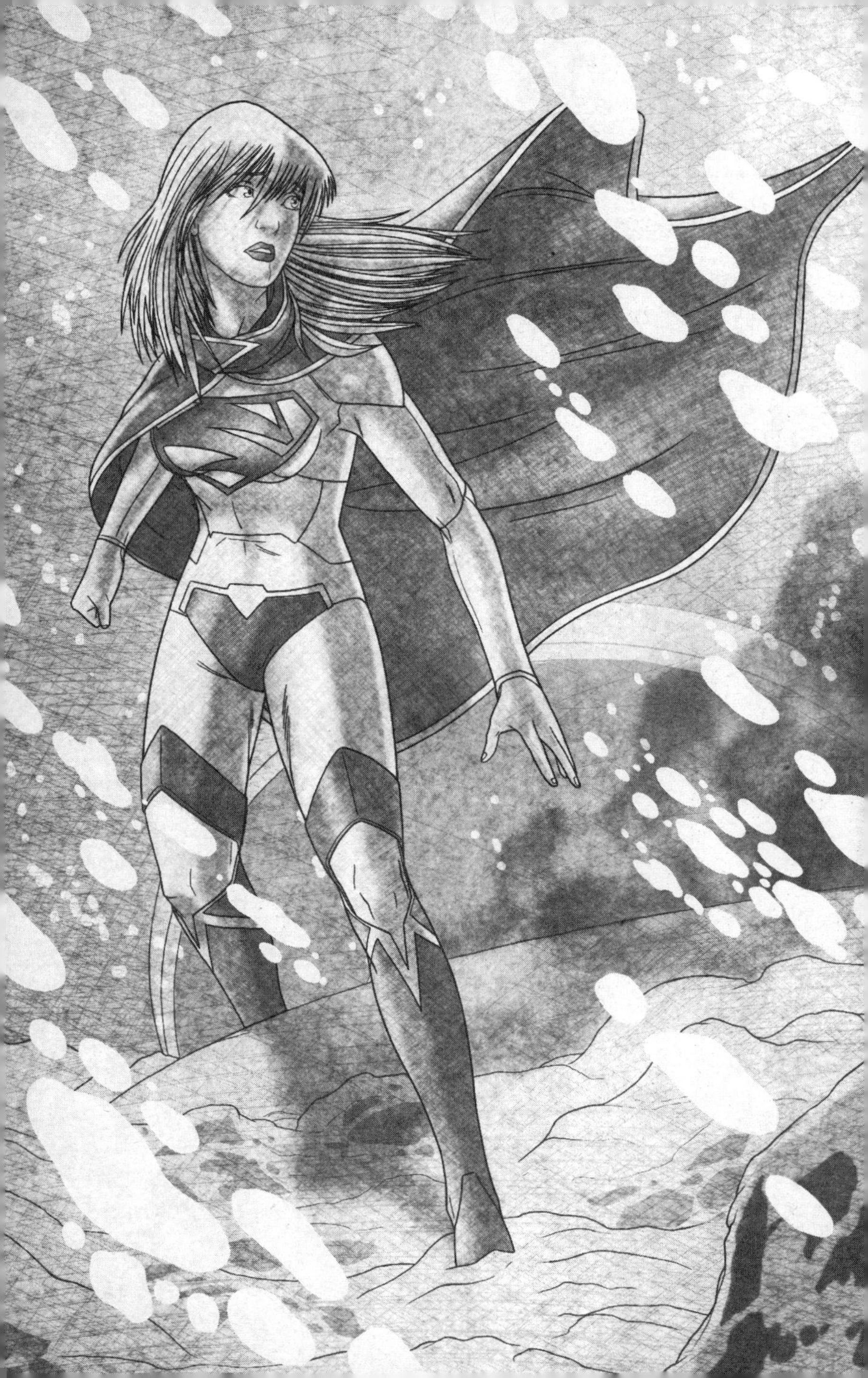

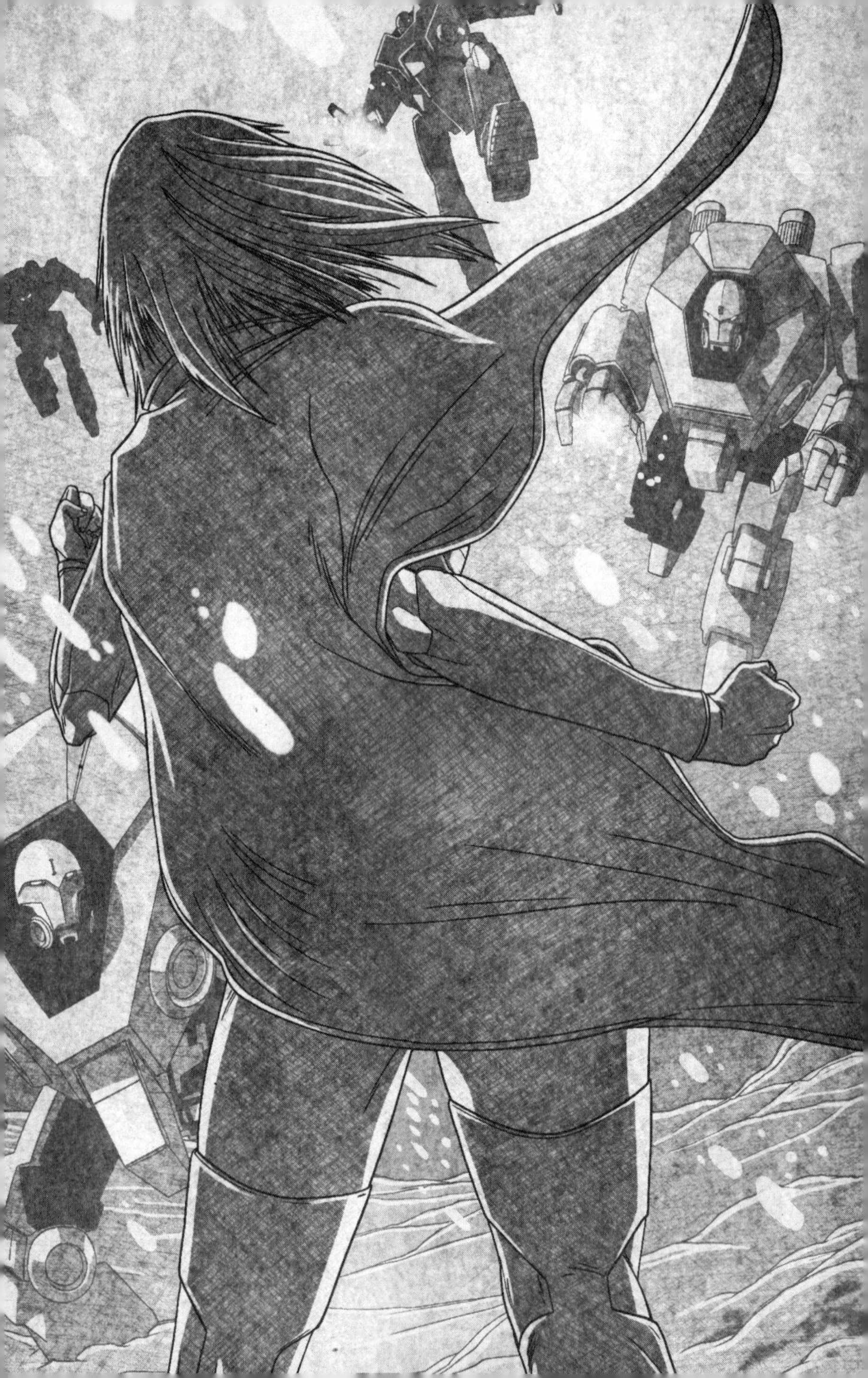

The lead armored figure stepped forward, shouting through a voice amplifier. Kara couldn't understand any of it. He was using a language that wasn't spoken anywhere on Krypton.

Kara extended her hand to show cooperation. To her shock, a blue tendril of energy shot from the soldier's gauntlet and wrapped around her forearm. Other soldiers did the same, binding Kara's other arm and both legs. When she struggled, the energy ropes squeezed tighter.

Far off on the horizon, the first light of sunrise illuminated the snowy plains. But this wasn't the familiar red disk of Rao that had shone on Krypton.

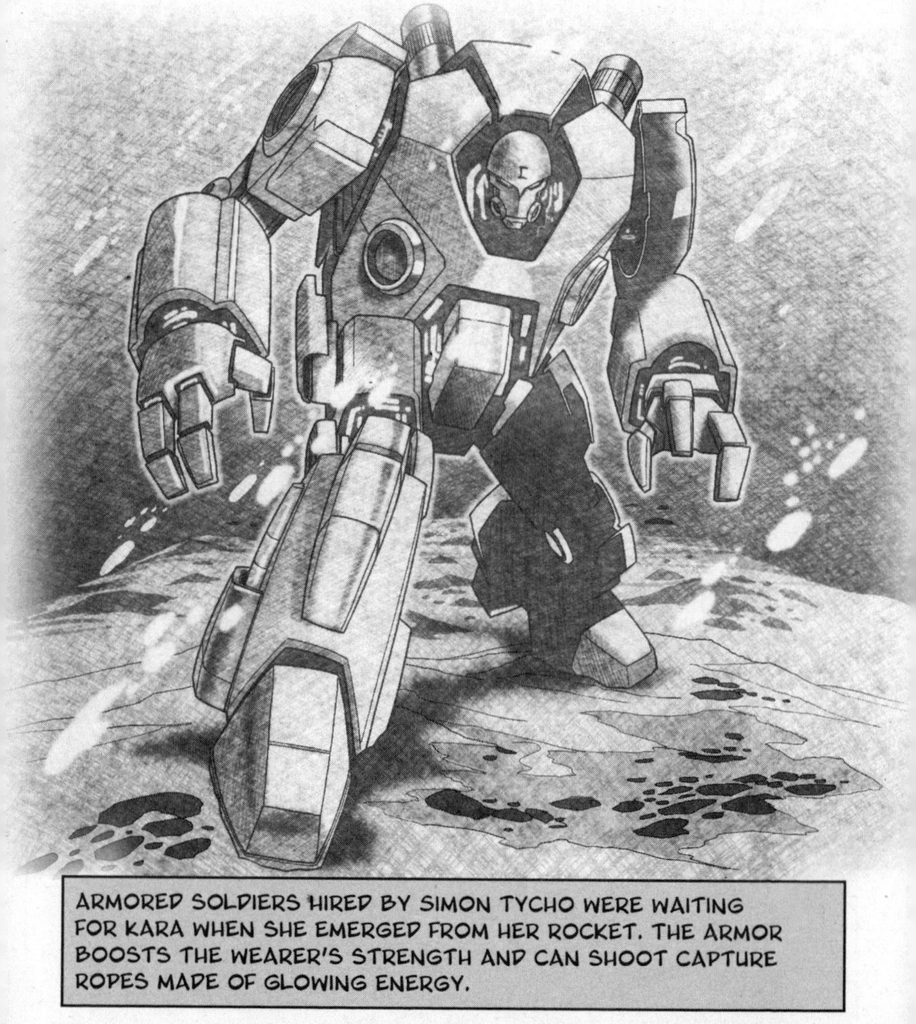

ARMORED SOLDIERS HIRED BY SIMON TYCHO WERE WAITING FOR KARA WHEN SHE EMERGED FROM HER ROCKET. THE ARMOR BOOSTS THE WEARER'S STRENGTH AND CAN SHOOT CAPTURE ROPES MADE OF GLOWING ENERGY.

This tiny ball gave off a pale yellow light that seemed to invigorate her despite the weakness of its rays.

This left no doubt—she wasn't on Krypton anymore. What was going on?

The lead soldier shouted again and tugged on his rope. Kara grew frightened. She couldn't remember where she was or what had happened to her parents, but she wasn't about to let a gang of strangers drag her off.

Kara yanked her arm back, tugging on the energy rope. "No!" she shouted in Kryptonian, and the frustration she felt inside suddenly exploded from her face. Twin beams of fire shot from her eyes, striking the lead soldier in the chest and knocking him over. On his armor, a small patch glowed white-hot where Kara's beams had hit.

A second soldier moved in close to tackle her. Kara shoved him, using a move she had practiced on her sparring robot only hours ago. To her astonishment her opponent sailed backward, arcing through the air before plowing to a halt a hundred meters away.

This didn't make any sense. What was happening to her body? Confused and starting to panic, she let out a scream of frustration. A ripple of sonic waves scattered the armored soldiers in every direction.

Breathing deeply to gather her inner calm, Kara prepared for another attack. Her father didn't like fighting, but Kara wasn't going to make herself an easy target. She brought her arms up into a ready stance, hands curled into fists.

"Stop!" came a voice from above. Kara realized with a shock that she understood. Someone was speaking Kryptonian. Kara craned her neck and squinted in the direction of the yellow sun.

Hovering in the air was a man she had never seen before, wearing blue, red, and yellow clothing that looked all too familiar. On his chest was the insignia of the House of El.

CHAPTER FOUR

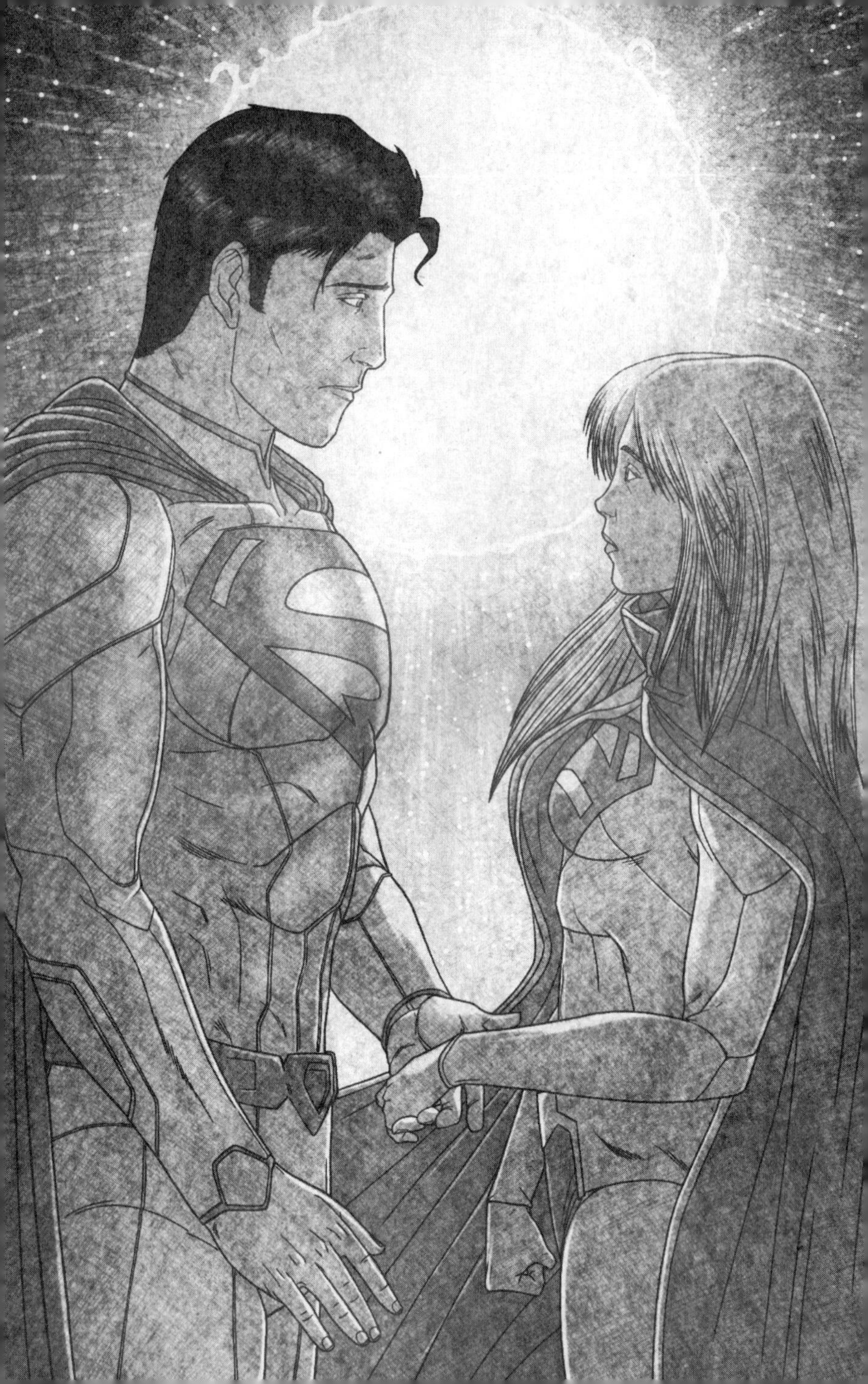

LEARNING THE TRUTH

The newcomer spoke using words she could understand, but he pronounced them clumsily and with a heavy accent. The armored soldiers had stopped their attack and were looking up at the man as if they recognized him. Was he their leader?

When he asked her to identify herself, Kara rattled off a rush of names—Kara Zor-El, Argo City, Krypton, Zor-El, Alura—in a challenging tone. To her surprise, the stranger reacted with recognition.

PROFILE

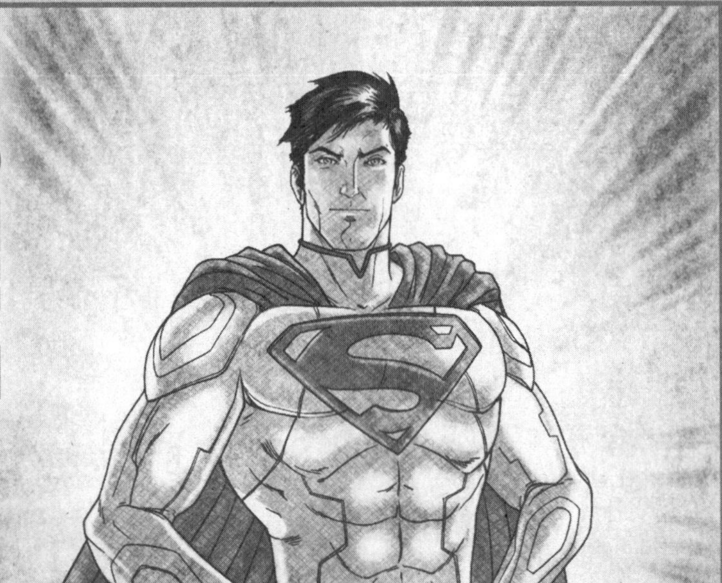

Kal-El (Superman)

On Krypton, Kal-El was Supergirl's baby cousin, the only child of her uncle Jor-El and her aunt Lara. Kal-El also escaped the destruction of Krypton inside a rocket, but he arrived on Earth right away instead of spending years in suspended animation. He grew up in Smallville, Kansas, under the care of his adoptive parents, Jonathan and Martha Kent, who called him Clark. By the time Supergirl finally arrived on Earth, Kal-El had already become Superman, the most famous Super Hero on Earth.

His father, Jor-El, had been Zor-El's brother, he explained, which would make them cousins. He introduced himself as Kal-El.

"Liar!" Kara shouted as her worst suspicions were confirmed. She swung her fist and was surprised when her blow knocked the stranger through a row of trees.

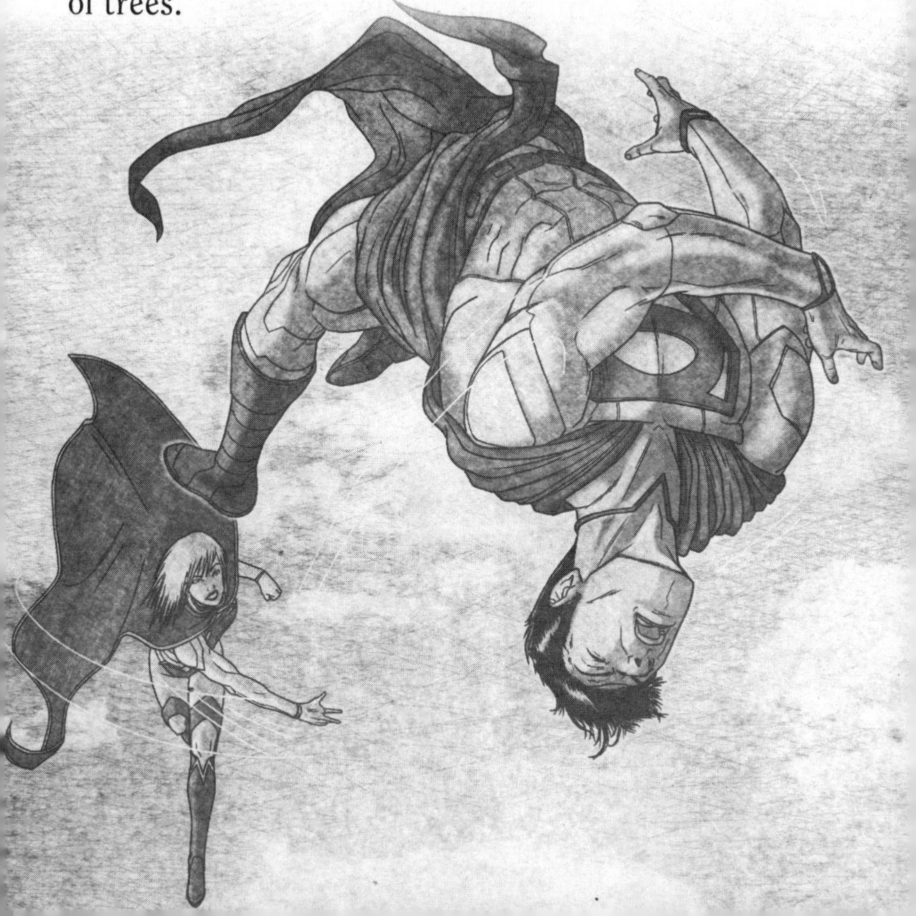

He was an impostor trying to trick her, Kara concluded. He couldn't be Kal-El. She had held Kal in her arms only days ago, and he was just a baby. Why couldn't she remember how she had arrived here? Did the impostor hold the answers?

She couldn't let him get away. Kara leapt forward and tackled him, straightening her fingers for a martial arts strike. When she glanced down at her hands, she no longer recognized them.

She could see *through* them—past the skin and all the way down to the muscles and bones. The stranger recognized Kara's confusion. He explained that this planet had given him similar powers, including a type of penetrating sight known as X-ray vision. Kara blinked and her eyesight returned to normal.

Kara was convinced that this must be another trick. He must be doing this to her. She rushed at the man, who fell backward and used Kara's momentum to launch her into the air.

Kara shot through a layer of clouds before she slowed and got her bearings. Beneath her feet, a patchy gray cloud bank stretched to the horizon. Above her head, the clear sky formed a peaceful blue dome. Kara took a moment, enjoying the sun on her skin, when suddenly the strangeness hit her all at once.

She was hovering in the air, under her own control.

She could fly!

The pure shock made her mental control collapse. Kara plunged toward the ground where the impostor caught her in his arms.

She pulled herself free, concentrating on how her mind had felt during her levitation. Her control snapped back. Kara willed herself to zoom just a few feet above the ground, listening to her cape flapping in the wind as she picked up speed. When Kara peered over her shoulder, she saw the stranger following her.

Kara flew faster, but the stranger kept up the pace. After crossing an immeasurable distance Kara brought herself to a stop. Below her, a long stone wall wound its way across a wooded mountain range. The wall looked old, and it definitely hadn't been built by Kryptonian hands.

The impostor spoke to her again. He explained that he believed that she was his cousin, Kara Zor-El, and he wanted to help her. "But the more you

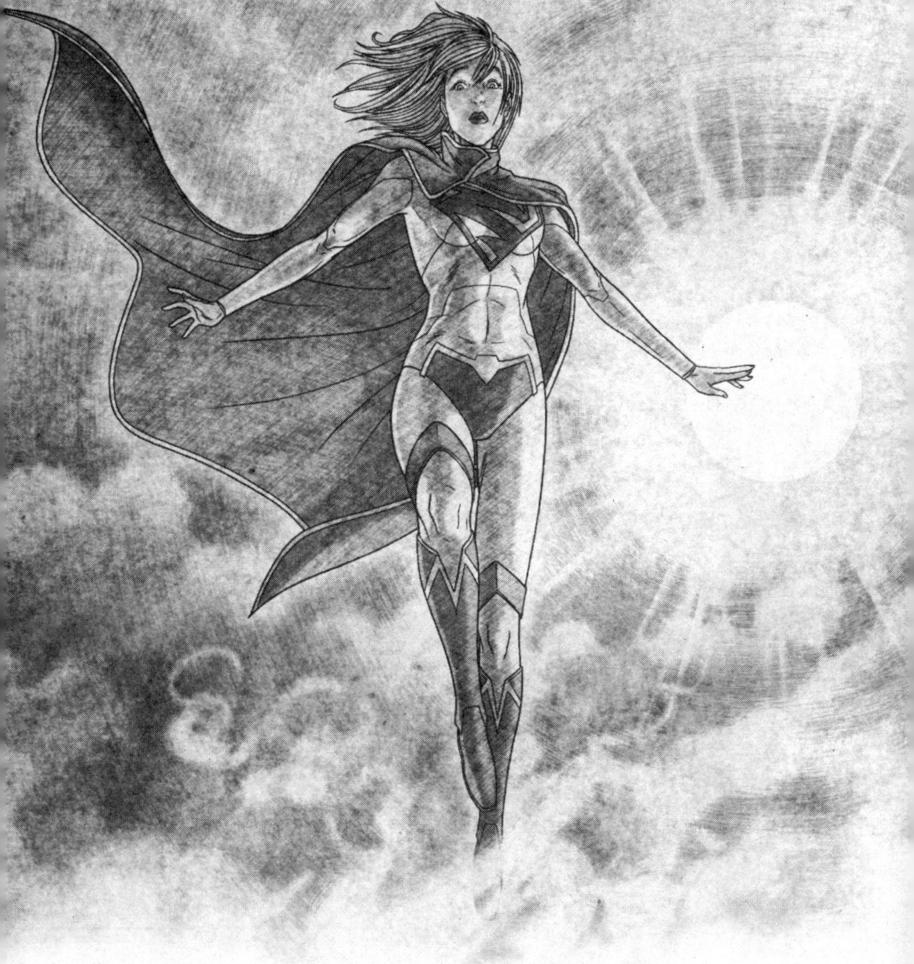

fight me," he pointed out, "the less I believe it's really you."

The comment stung. Kara realized that she had been acting irrationally, preferring to fight instead of reason. The only thing she had accomplished was to make the stranger suspicious of her, too.

Clearing her mind, she took a fresh look at the facts. In the stranger's face she saw the features of her uncle Jor-El. In his blue eyes she saw her baby cousin looking back at her. It was true. He *was* Kal-El.

Kara remained quiet as Kal told his story. Jor-El and Lara had sent him in a rocket to the planet Earth, where human parents had raised him as Clark Kent. He didn't discover the amazing powers given to him by Earth's yellow sun until he was a teenager.

Once he understood his powers, he vowed to use his abilities to protect the people of Earth.

Kal-El gestured to a crowd of people gathered atop the stone wall. This was the Great Wall of China, he explained, and these were the people of Earth. They knew him, and they called him "Superman."

Earth was his home now, he continued, and Earth would become her home, too. She had no other choice.

Krypton was gone forever.

CHAPTER FIVE

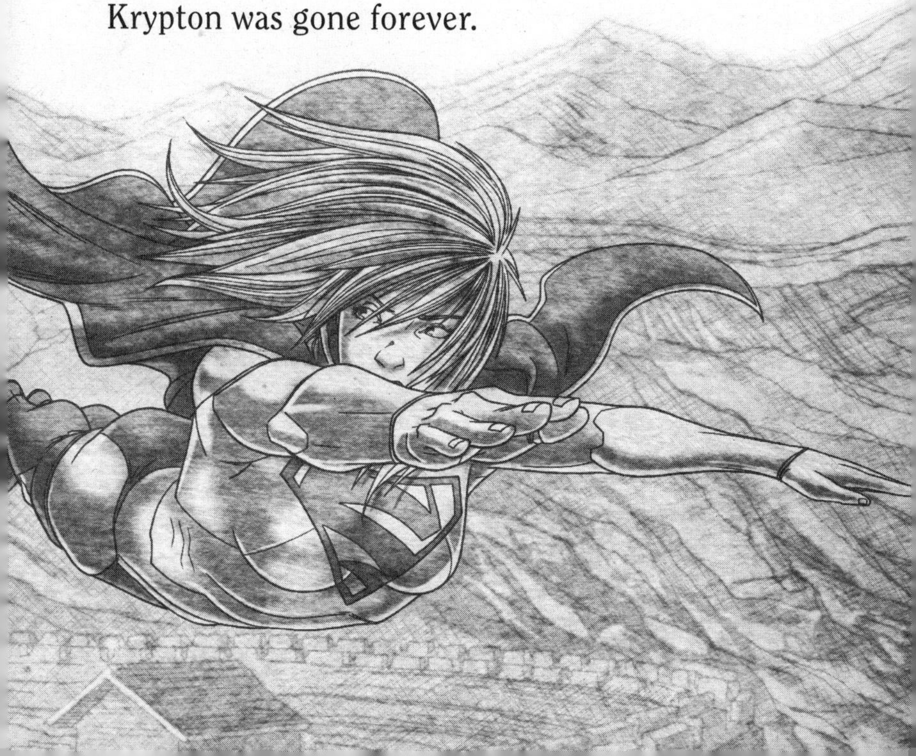

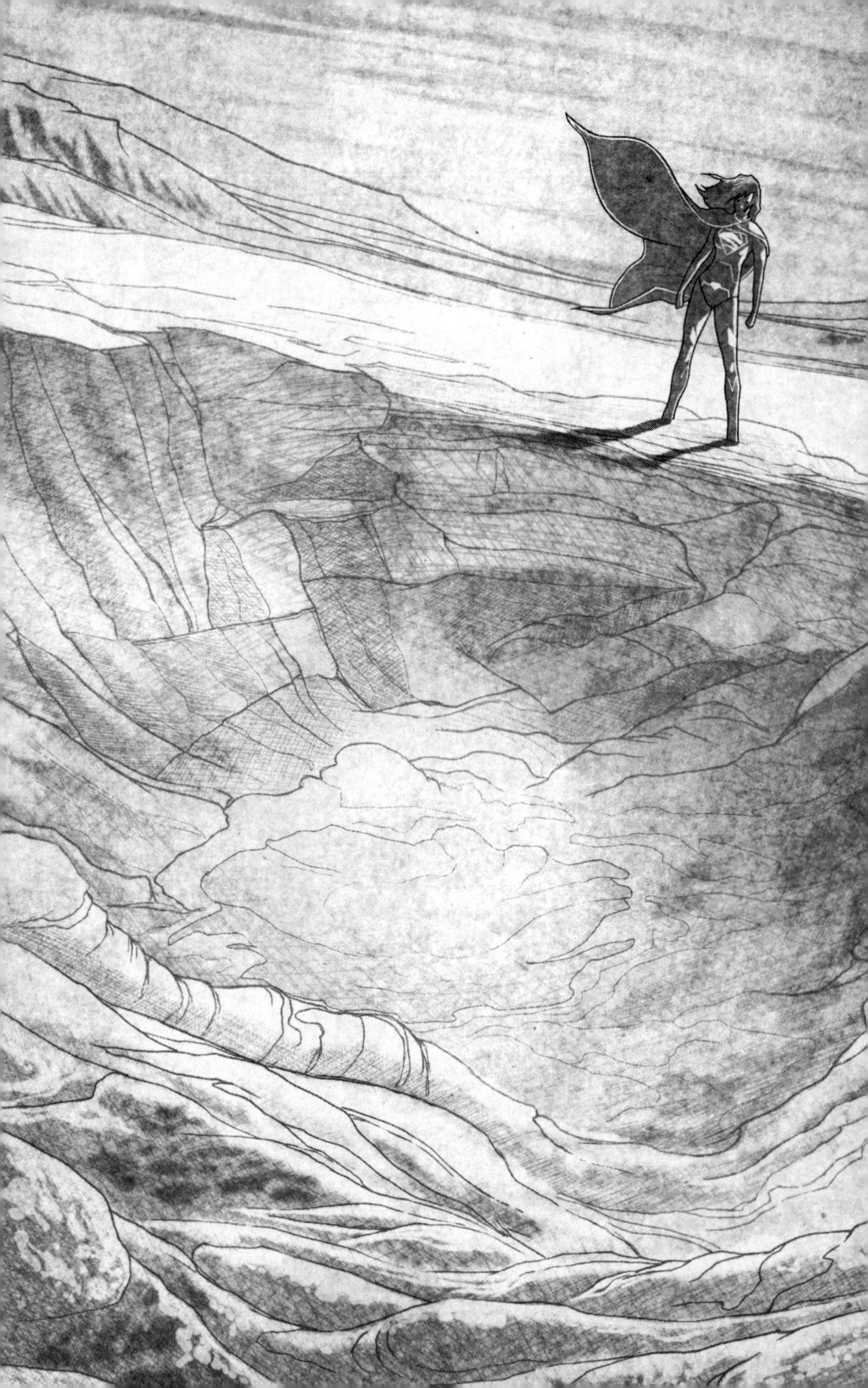

POWER
TESTING

Kara gasped, and foggy memories suddenly began to take shape in her mind. Her father, and the rocket, and ... Without a word, Kara launched into the sky and raced off at a blistering speed.

Could Krypton really be gone? Kara clung to the hope that Kal didn't know all the facts. Perhaps if she investigated the rocket that had carried her to this planet she might find some clue that Kal had overlooked. Kara retraced her path, arriving at the site of her crash landing.

The rocket was nowhere to be found—only the empty crater remained. Kara frantically scanned her surroundings. A holographic image abruptly shimmered to life, portraying a young man with intelligent but cruel eyes. He spoke to her in a language she didn't recognize, but he seemed to give his name as Simon Tycho. Smiling coldly, the man brought a new image into view: Kara's rocket.

He'd stolen it. As the man concluded his speech, Kara looked around for the source of the hologram and identified a hovering metal ball. When it rose into the sky, Kara followed.

The hologram projector rose higher and higher, passing through the atmosphere and into the vacuum of space. Kara stayed glued to its tail. Eventually the silvery orb reached an orbiting space station and disappeared inside through a tiny hatch.

Realizing that she wasn't sure how much longer she could hold her breath out in space, Kara

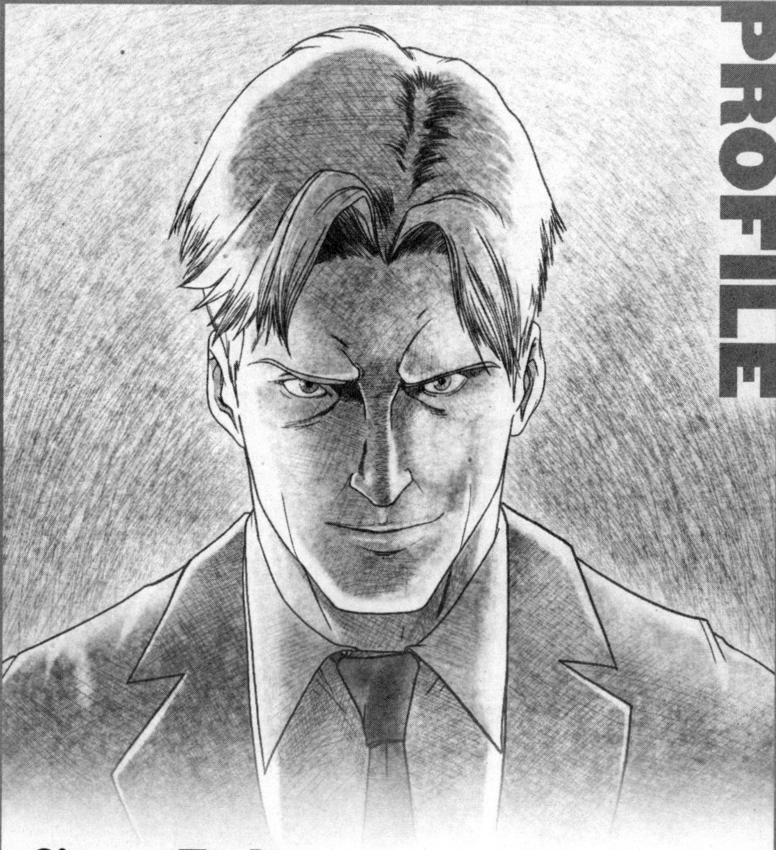
PROFILE

Simon Tycho

One of the richest and smartest people on Earth, Simon Tycho is also one of the most ruthless. He made his fortune by stealing corporate secrets and conducting unsafe scientific experiments. His headquarters is a space station that orbits the planet, allowing him to keep an eye on all the world's nations without having to obey any of their laws. When he learns that another Kryptonian like Superman has arrived on Earth, Simon Tycho does everything he can to uncover her secrets.

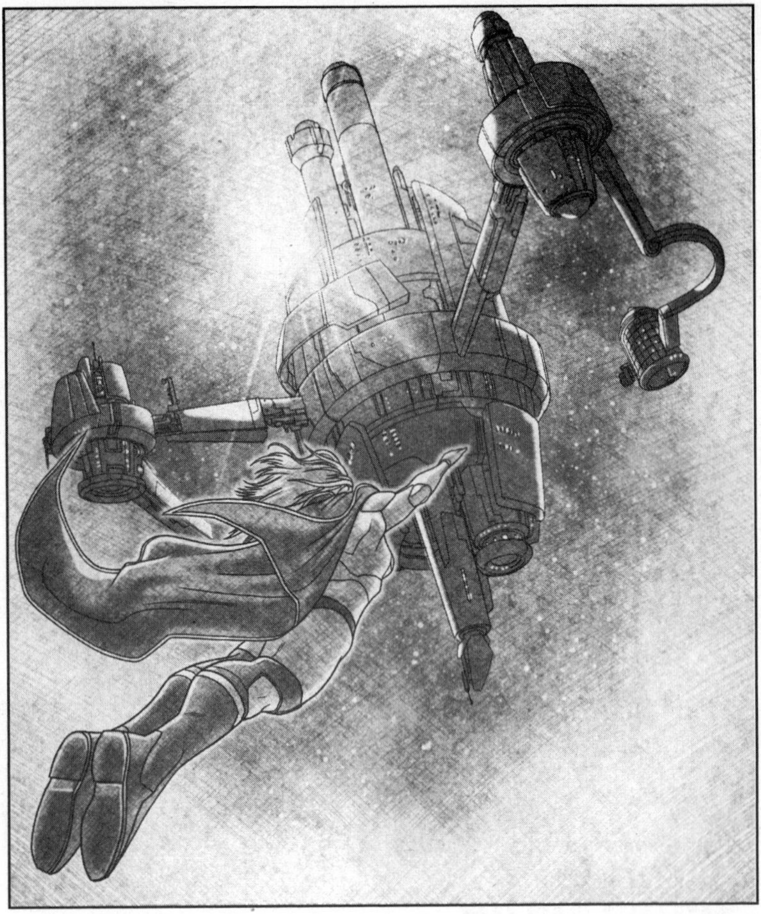

approached the station's main air lock. It sealed shut behind her, and Kara filled her lungs with the stale taste of recycled air. With her X-ray vision she saw devices and machines filling nearly every corner of the station. Kara didn't know all of their functions, but having grown up in a family of scientists, she knew testing equipment when she saw it. If Simon Tycho was a scientist, Kara concluded that she was supposed to be his next experiment.

Kara stepped into an open chamber and a swarm of metal cylinders no bigger than her finger dropped from the ceiling. Each cylinder unfolded a pair of silvery wings. The strange constructions buzzed around her head, just like the insects that circled the Argo Lightbridge at sunset. Kara reached out to touch one, and it zapped her hand with a beam of green energy.

THESE SMALL, INSECTLIKE ROBOTS FIRE ENERGY BEAMS AND CAN COORDINATE SWARM ATTACKS IN WHICH THEY ALL STRIKE A SINGLE TARGET AT THE SAME TIME.

Kara cried out, wincing and tucking her arms against her body as more beams stabbed at her skin. The needlelike zaps didn't seem to be causing any lasting injury, but they hurt just the same. Angry at the unprovoked attack, Kara felt her emotion taking form as a warm ball in her chest. It radiated out to her skin and crawled all the way down to the tips of her fingers and toes. Kara's skin shimmered with burning heat. The swarm of metal fliers glowed red and dropped to the floor, wings melted and sagging.

Kara strode with confidence into the next chamber, where a different threat awaited. A translucent, jellylike creature reached its arms around her shoulders, pulling its rubbery body next to hers. Kara fought, but her fists sunk uselessly into the thick goo. The monster oozed closer to her face. Soon, she wouldn't be able to breathe.

Getting a quick read of her surroundings, Kara propelled herself and the monster toward the nearest wall—punching straight through it until

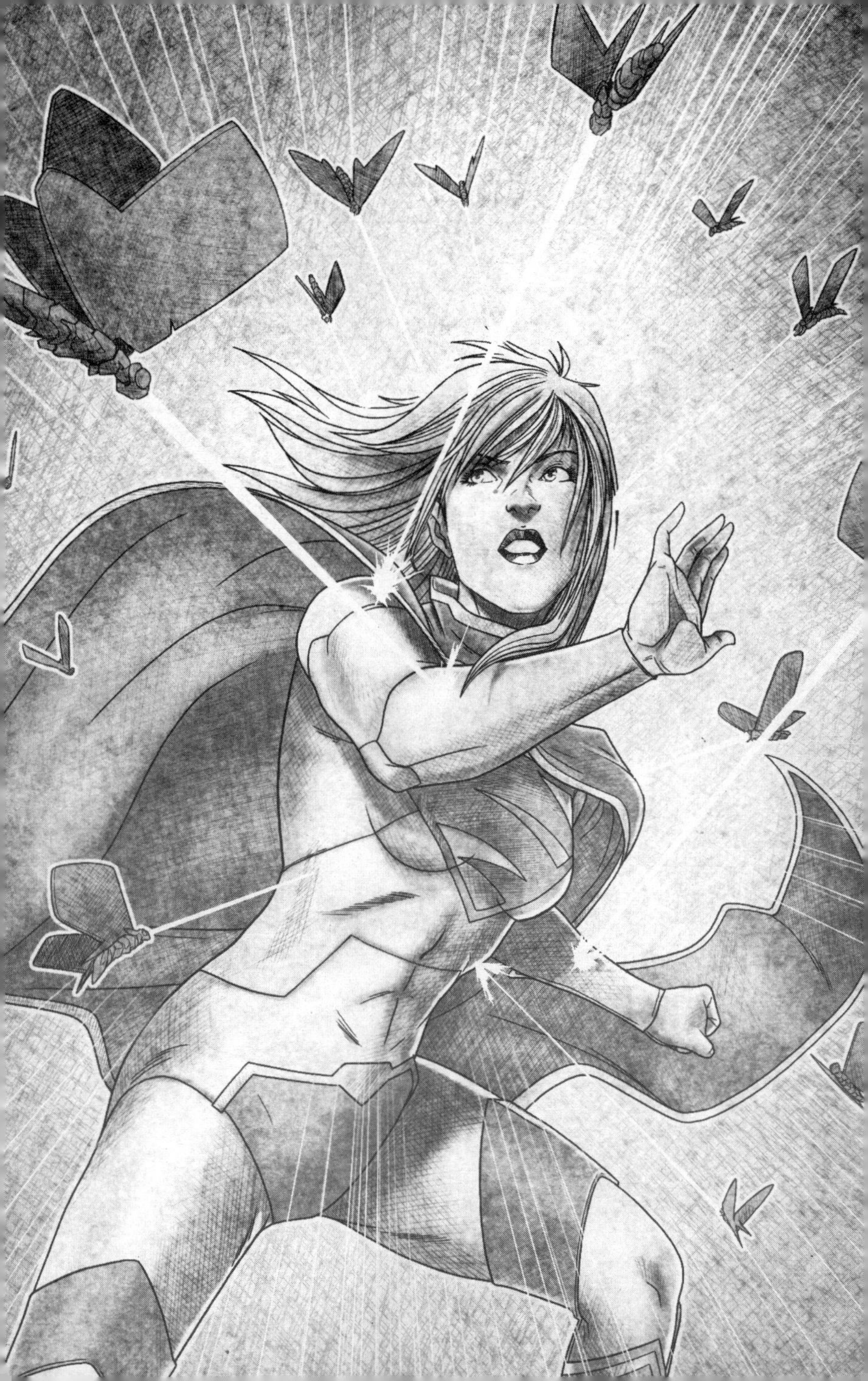

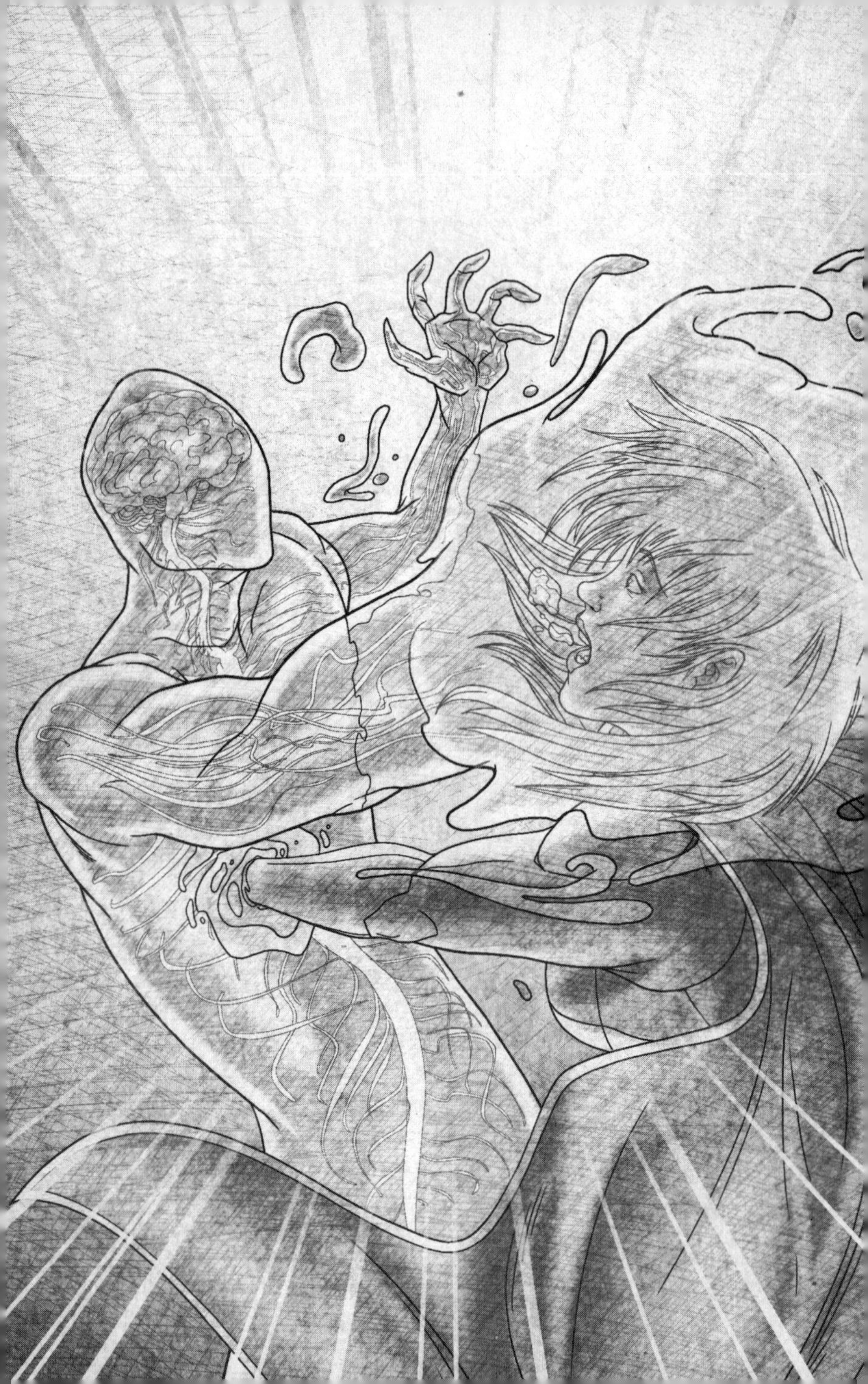

she had reached the cold emptiness of outer space. The creature froze solid as a statue.

Kara stormed back into the main lab. Her rocket sat in an examination bay, its shell cracked and its inner workings open for inspection. Simon Tycho saw Kara but didn't try to stop her as she reached the spacecraft. He knew he couldn't outfight her, and based on her recent performance he was probably having serious doubts on whether he could outthink her.

From her rocket, Kara retrieved a single artifact: a palm-sized crystal glowing with a soft inner light. On Krypton, these sunstones stored important data.

If a sunstone had been placed inside her rocket, it must contain information that she was meant to see. Maybe it could reveal what had really happened to Krypton.

CHAPTER SIX

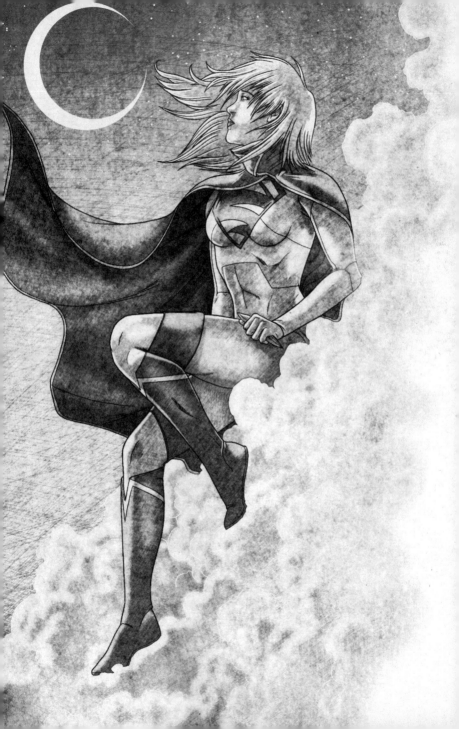

SEARCHING FOR ANSWERS

Kara hovered in the night sky, gazing up at the stars. She couldn't bring herself to land back on Earth, not again. What could this planet offer her?

So far, everyone she had met either wanted to fight or perform experiments on her. They seemed okay with Kal-El, but maybe that was because he had grown up among them. Kara didn't know how to relate to these new people. How could she make her home on an alien world?

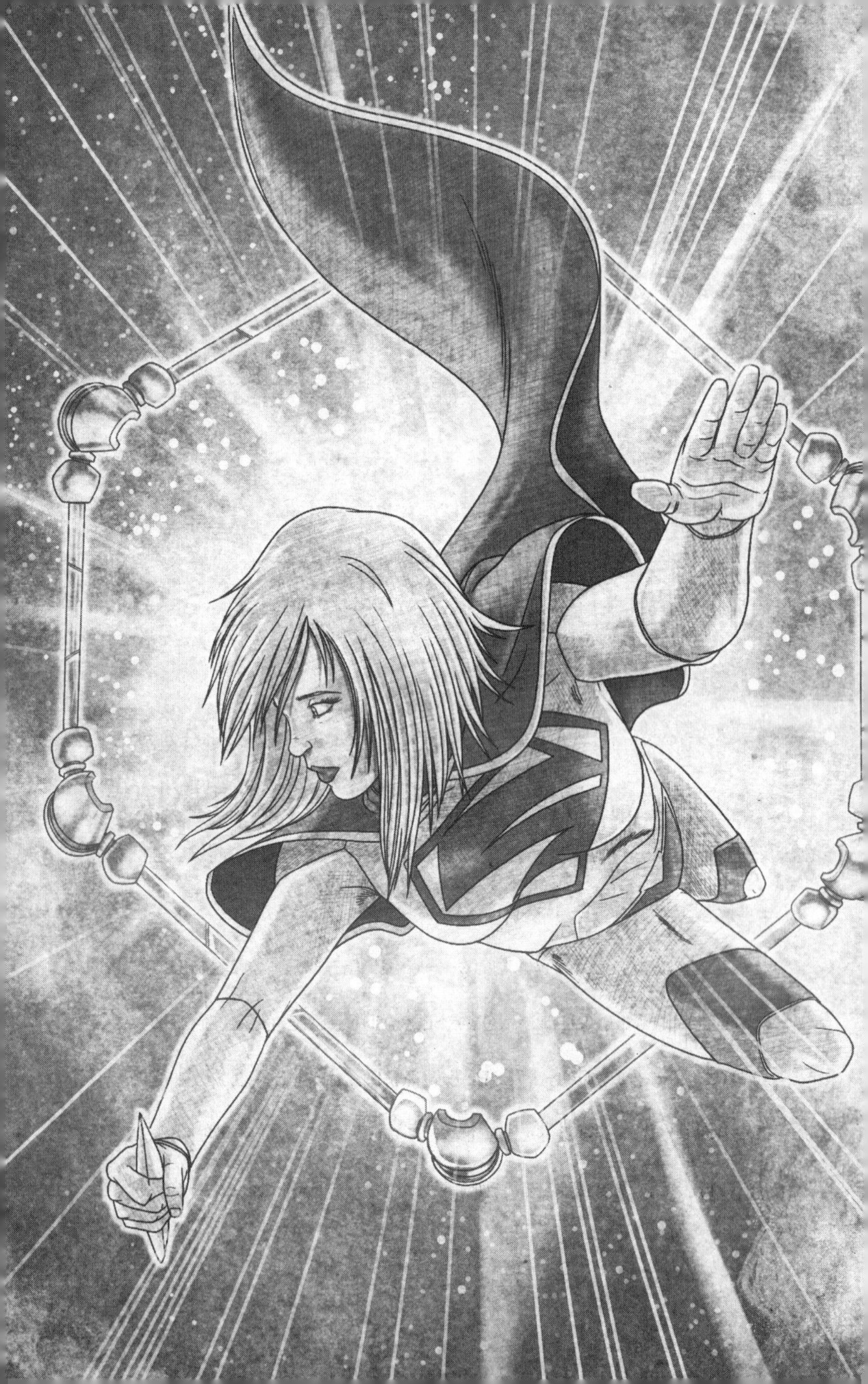

There was only one thing to do: go back to Krypton. Kal-El had insisted it was gone, but what evidence did he really have? The sunstone, a miniaturized wonder of Kryptonian technology, could open a wormhole between any two points in the galaxy, and Kara had already proven she could survive in space without a ship. Taking one last look at Earth, Kara soared up toward the waiting stars.

The sunstone had been manufactured on Krypton and instinctively knew the coordinates of the planet's last known location. Kara shivered as she passed through the wormhole, but the transition lasted only an instant. When she emerged on the other side, Argo City lay before her.

But it wasn't Argo City—not as she remembered it. Familiar buildings covered one side of a massive asteroid. The opposite side was jagged and rocky, as if the asteroid had been torn loose in an explosion. Kara's heart sank as she realized that was exactly what had happened.

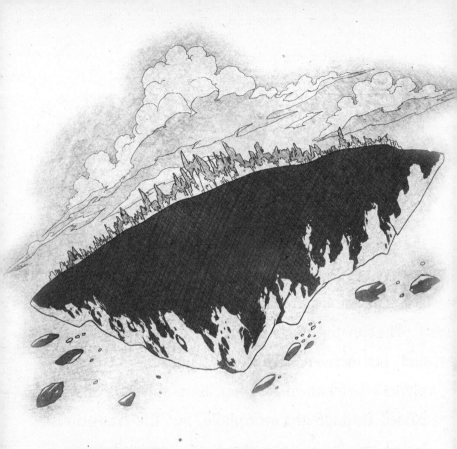

She remembered now. She remembered how her father had believed that the power generators surrounding Argo City might generate a force field and protect its citizens from the explosion of Krypton. It appeared that the force field had worked, but only partially. Argo City remained intact but its buildings were shattered, broken . . . and empty.

Kal-El was right. Krypton was gone.

Kara flew in close, feeling numb as her eyes took in the ghost town that remained. The multicolored mosses of the Infinity Gardens had been burned

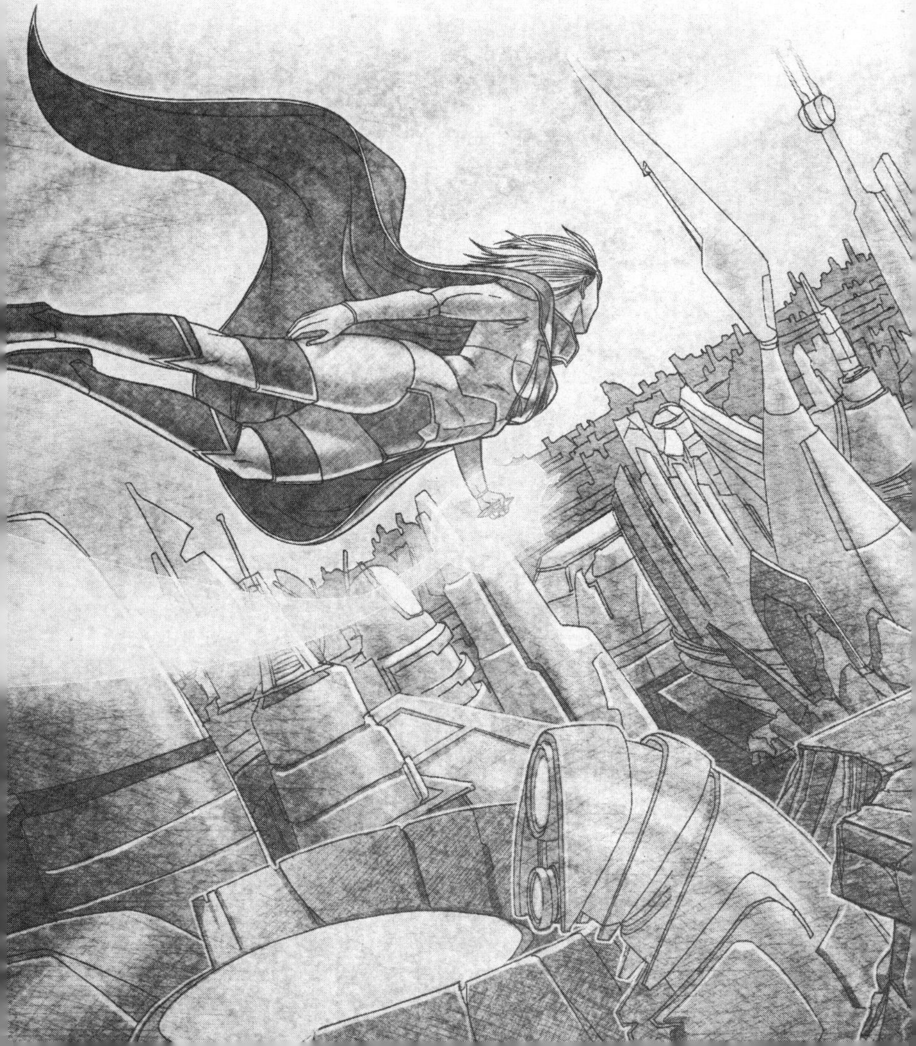

away, leaving only trails of ash. The Hope Spire had crumbled to the ground. The firefalls no longer flowed, and the few pools of liquid left in the river basin had almost completely evaporated.

Home was her first stop. Kara's sparring robot sat lifeless in one corner. A thin layer of dust covered the table where her family had shared meals. The silence felt overwhelming, especially with the extra-sensitive hearing she had gained through exposure to the yellow sun of Earth.

Kara lingered in the doorway to the courtyard. She had stood in the same spot just days ago—or at least, it felt like days. Kara now knew that many years had passed since she had last set foot on Krypton.

In Zor-El's secret laboratory, the memories came flooding back. Those hoisting claws had held her rocket. That room was where she had tried on her Kryptonian outfit for the first time. Kara looked down at the crest of the House of El on her chest. Now who would carry on her family's legacy? It

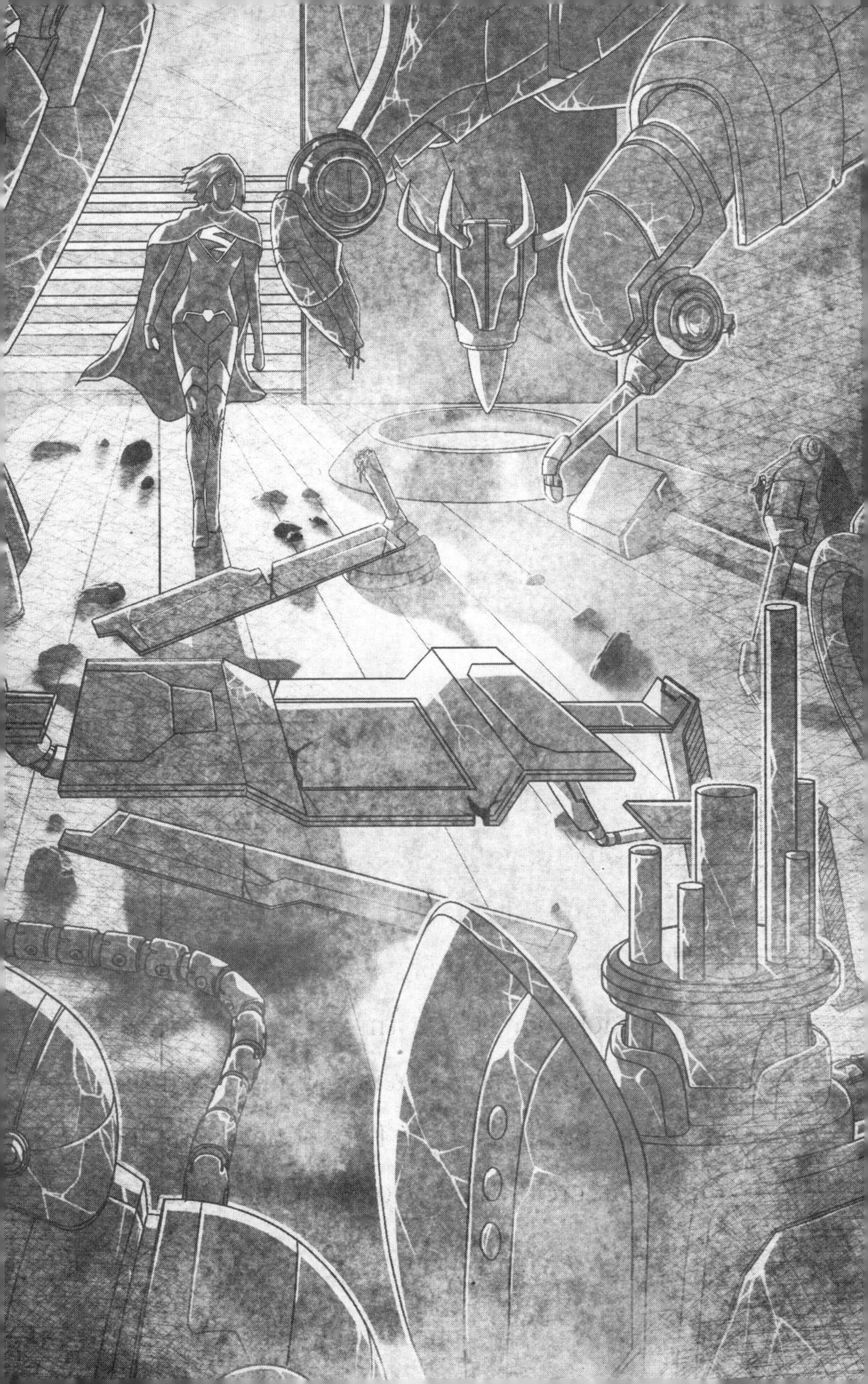

couldn't be Kal, not when he had only lived in this world as a baby.

Kara realized, with a mix of sadness and pride, that she was the last true Kryptonian.

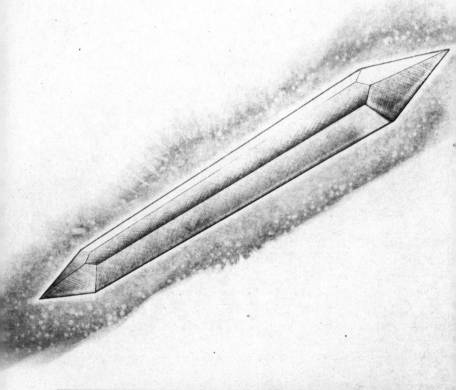

A KRYPTONIAN SUNSTONE IS A CRYSTAL THAT STORES INFORMATION, AND ALSO HAS OTHER HIDDEN ABILITIES. KARA'S FATHER PLACED A SUNSTONE INSIDE HER ROCKET BEFORE HER ESCAPE FROM KRYPTON.

Kara plugged her sunstone into the lab's workstation. A hologram of Zor-El snapped into view. Kara listened to his words, but she no longer cared about information. She had accepted the truth. Now she only wanted to hear her father's voice one last time.

As Kara left the lab, her ears detected an impossible sound. Soft footsteps were drawing near. Could someone else have survived Argo City's ruin? Her thoughts were interrupted when a tall woman—her dark eyes and gray skin marking her as an alien—grabbed Kara and roughly pinned her against a wall.

She announced herself as Reign, and explained that she also possessed superpowers. Her abilities, however, had come from Kryptonian military science. Reign was a Worldkiller, a living weapon created to serve and conquer. But her commanders had died, and there was nothing left in Argo City to conquer.

PROFILE

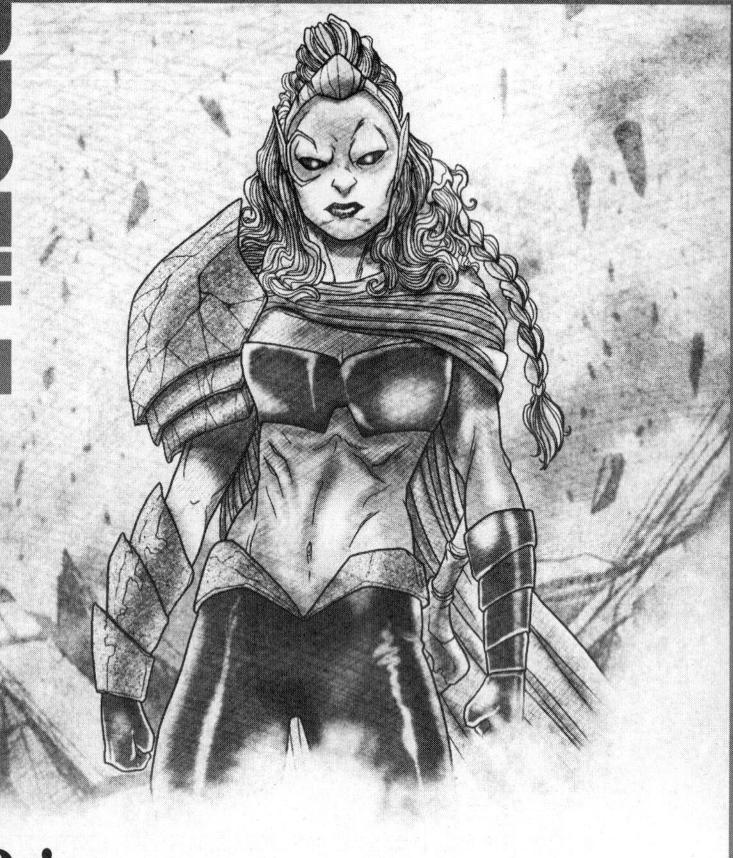

Reign

Reign is a mighty warrior created—along with other aliens known as Worldkillers—to serve the military of Krypton. She and the other Worldkillers had no one to serve when Krypton exploded, and Reign realized that her superpowers could make her an unbeatable conqueror. Her abilities include amazing strength and blinding-fast speed, but her greatest talent is her skill with military tactics. Reign is a natural leader, and she quickly organized the Worldkillers into a fighting force with the goal of taking over Earth.

Reign could see that Kara was strong. She assumed that she must be a warrior, too. With a cruel smile, she invited Kara to join her in achieving a great victory. If she couldn't rule the dead world of Krypton, Reign declared, then she would take control of Earth.

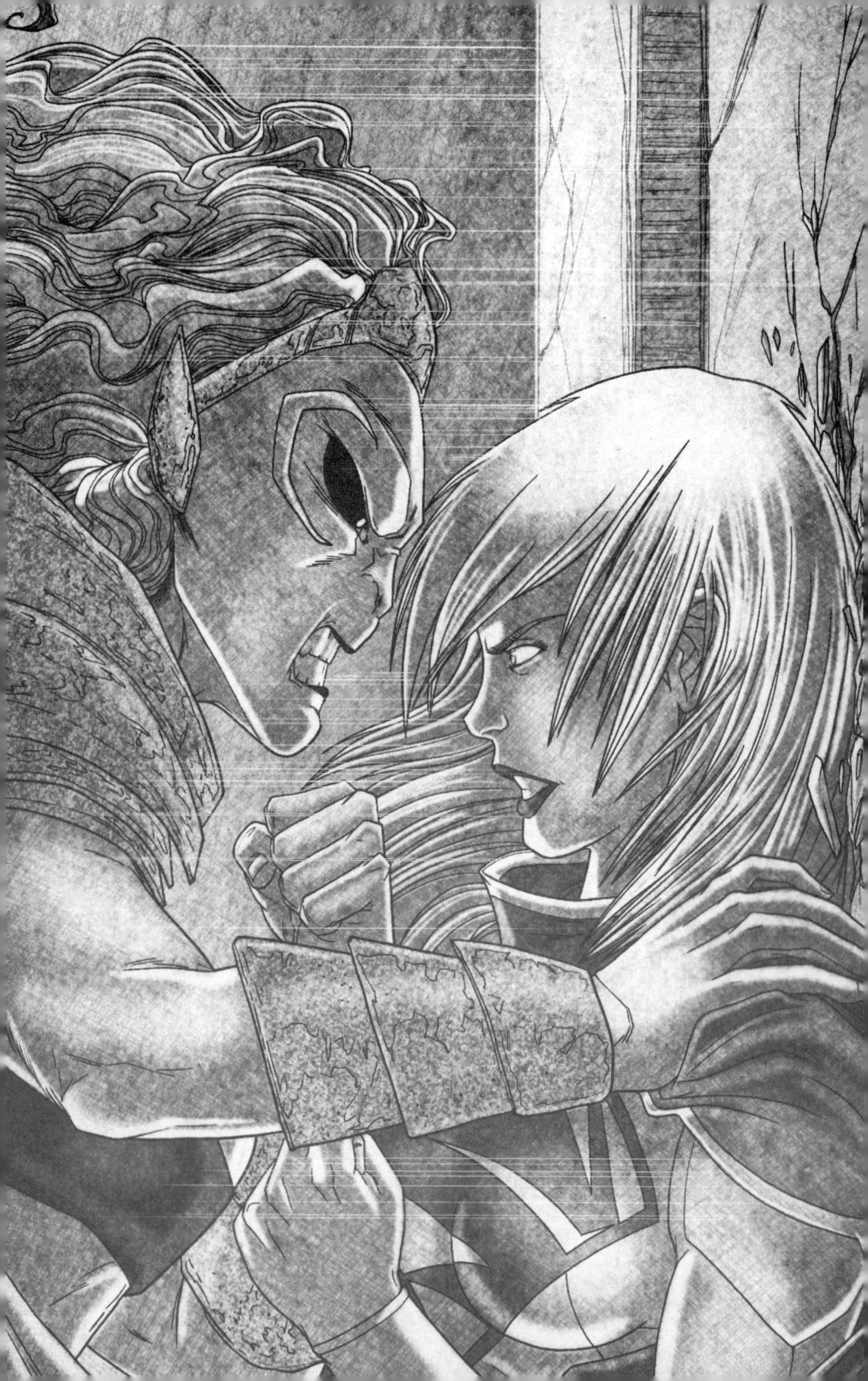

CHAPTER SEVEN

KARA AGAINST THE WORLDKILLERS

Kara recoiled at Reign's invitation. Despite the anguish she felt from losing everything she had ever known, the thought of causing even more pain to others made her sick to her stomach. Reign snarled at this unexpected response, calling Kara weak and cowardly. With a final grunt of disgust, Reign turned and left.

Kara slumped to the ground. Her shoulder ached where Reign had pinned her against the wall. It was the first time Kara had faced an opponent who was as strong as she was and who wasn't holding back. With a stab of fear, Kara realized that Reign was strong enough to end her life.

She couldn't go to back to Earth, not even to fight the threat posed by Reign. The people of Earth didn't want her there. If she faced Reign she might get badly injured, or worse.

But who else could stop Reign? Kal-El had the power, but he didn't understand Krypton's history like Kara did. Kal also didn't have a lifetime of Kryptonian scientific education, with hands-on experience in logic and problem solving.

Her father had valued her scientific training far more than her physical training. Still, there was something that Zor-El always said, every time Kara took a strong hit from her sparring robot: "If you get knocked down, get back up."

Kara rose shakily to her feet. Before her, she saw images of her father and mother. These were not holograms; they were Kara's memories. Their shared life on Argo City was something that Kara could never get back, but Zor-El and Alura would live on as long as Kara remembered them.

"Your mother and I are here for you, Kara," said Zor-El. "We will always be here for you."

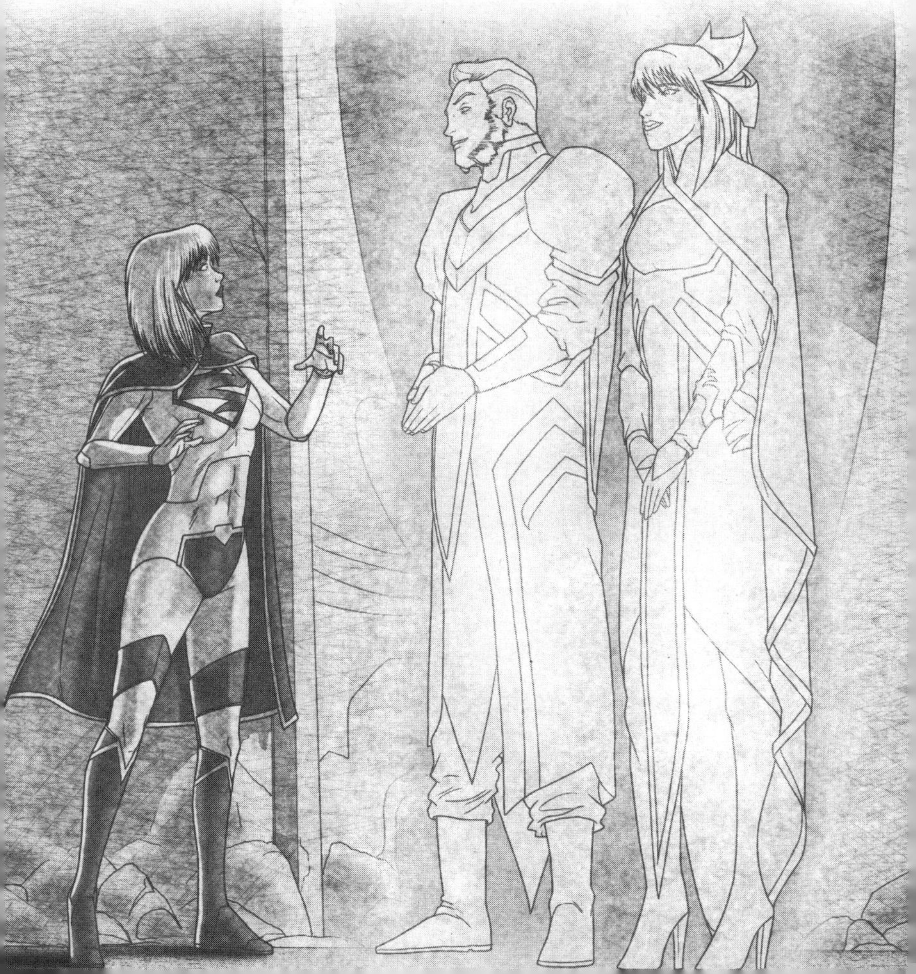

Alura extended both arms, her face radiating kindness and humor. "You have the power, Kara, it is always inside you," she said. "It will never leave your heart, as you never left ours."

Above the planet Earth, a wormhole shimmered. Out of it shot a newly determined Kara Zor-El. Her old life was gone, and she had only one place left to go. If Reign wanted to hurt others on her new home, then it was up to Kara to stop her.

Reign had landed in the heat of a busy city called New York. As Kara flew closer, she saw that Reign had brought backup.

Reign's three accomplices, she explained to Kara, were also Kryptonian Worldkillers. Flower of Heaven, a being of pure energy, could fire destructive beams from her containment suit. The tusk-faced Deimax could generate earthquakes. Perrilus was a sharp-toothed reptile who liked to inject poison with her stabbing tentacles.

Kara wasted no time, flying straight for the

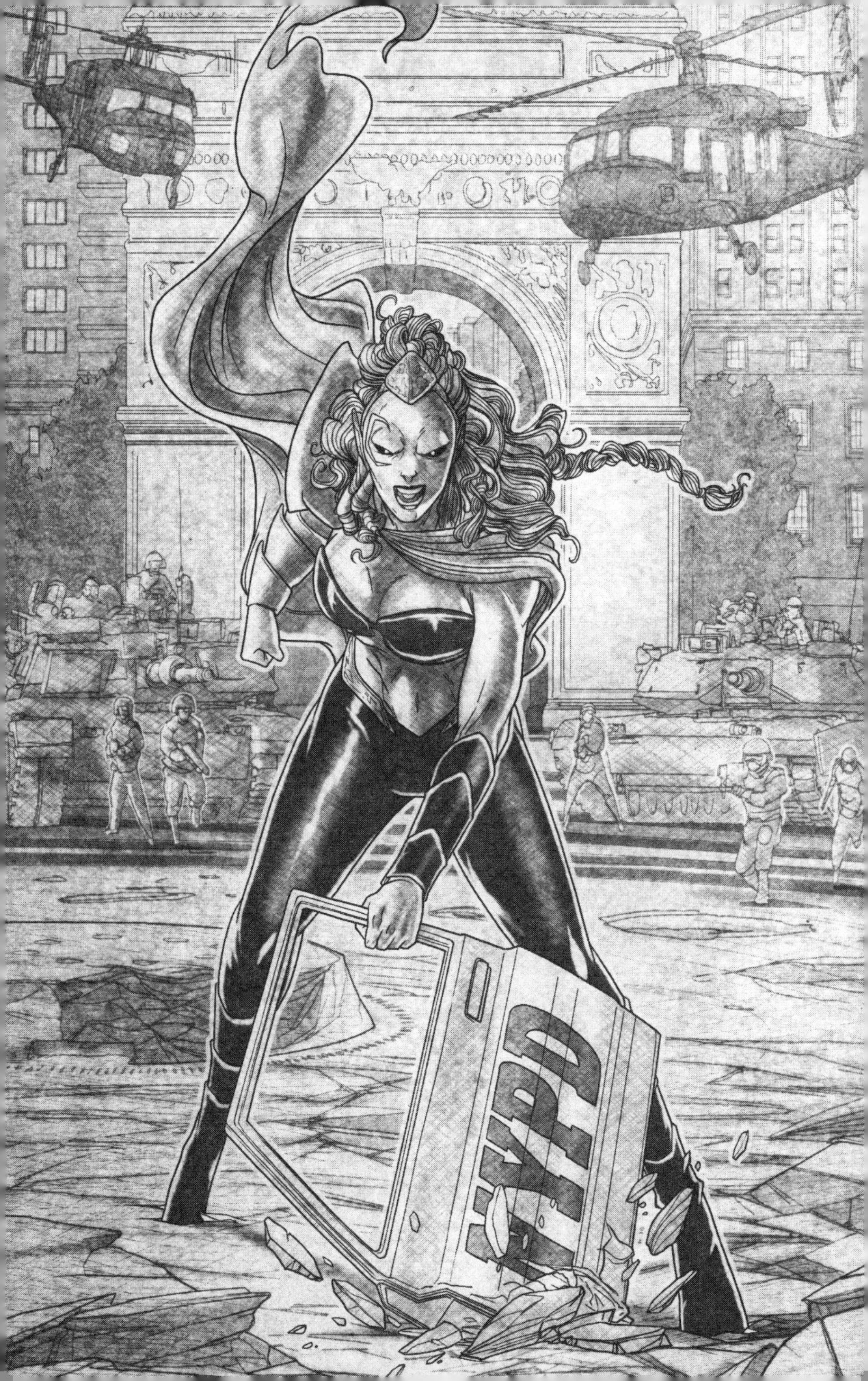
NYPD

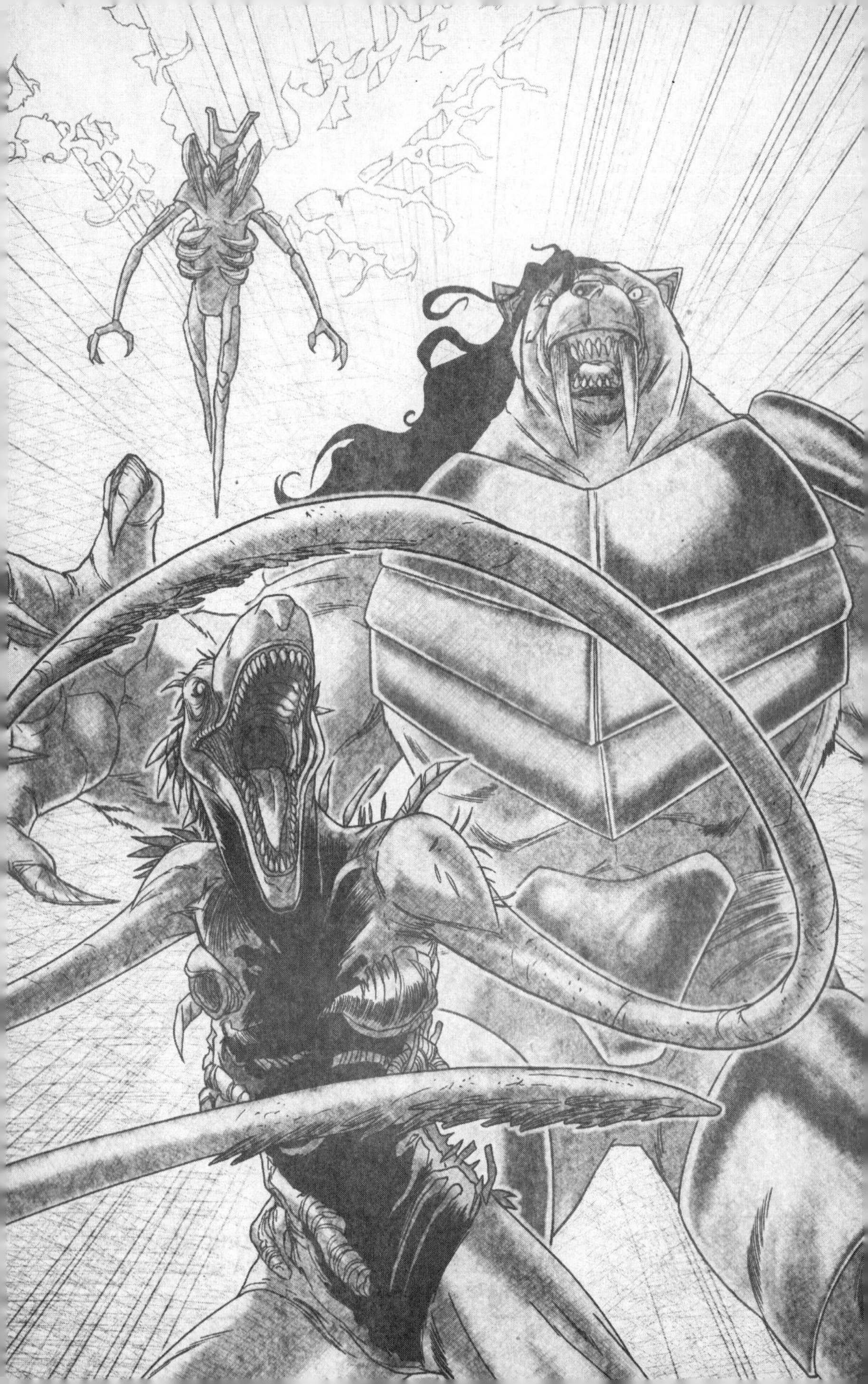

Worldkillers before they could attack the crowds of awestruck New Yorkers gathered on the sidewalks. Deimax grabbed Kara and pulled her into a tight armlock. Kara raised the temperature of her skin, and Deimax roared as the heat singed her fur.

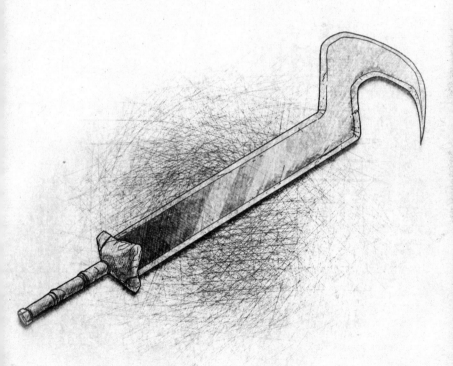

THIS SWORD WAS CARRIED BY REIGN, THE SUPERPOWERED LEADER OF THE WORLDKILLERS. THE KRYPTONIAN MILITARY TRAINED HER IN THE USE OF SWORDS AND OTHER DANGEROUS WEAPONS.

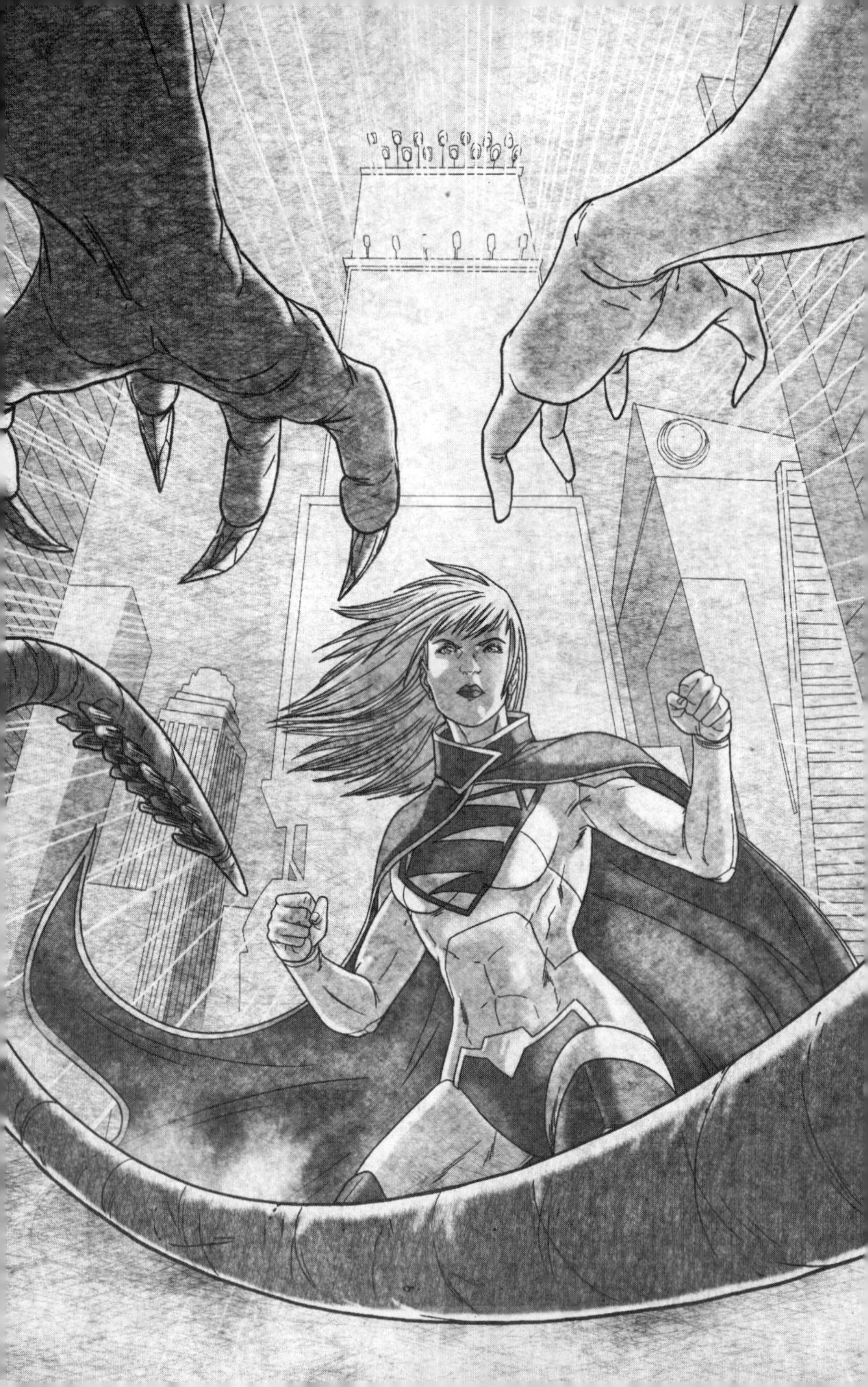

Remembering her training sessions, Kara scanned her enemies and evaluated their positions. She moved in toward Flower of Heaven, using super-strength to pry open her containment shell and release the energy that allowed her to hold her shape. Already anticipating a sneaky strike from Perrilus, Kara ducked and grabbed her tentacles instead, redirecting them right into Deimax's chest. Deimax fell to the ground, already feeling the sickening effects of Perrilus's poison.

Reign's team had lost, and she knew she couldn't win the day on her own. The Worldkillers departed, but not before Reign promised Kara that she was in for an even bigger fight next time.

Kara looked around, struggling to catch her breath. Hundreds of humans were looking at her. In their eyes she saw a mix of emotions ranging from suspicion to relief. Many of them—especially the children—smiled when they saw the House of El symbol on her uniform.

None of them could read Kryptonian, and none of them would ever understand what the symbol meant to Kara. But on Earth the symbol had come to mean something else. It stood for hope. When Kal-El wore it, it was an *S* for Superman. Kara listened closely to the chatter of the crowd, picking out several voices that whispered to each other the name "Supergirl."

Maybe life here wouldn't be so bad. She would always be Kara Zor-El of Krypton. Now she could also become Supergirl of Earth.

CHAPTER EIGHT

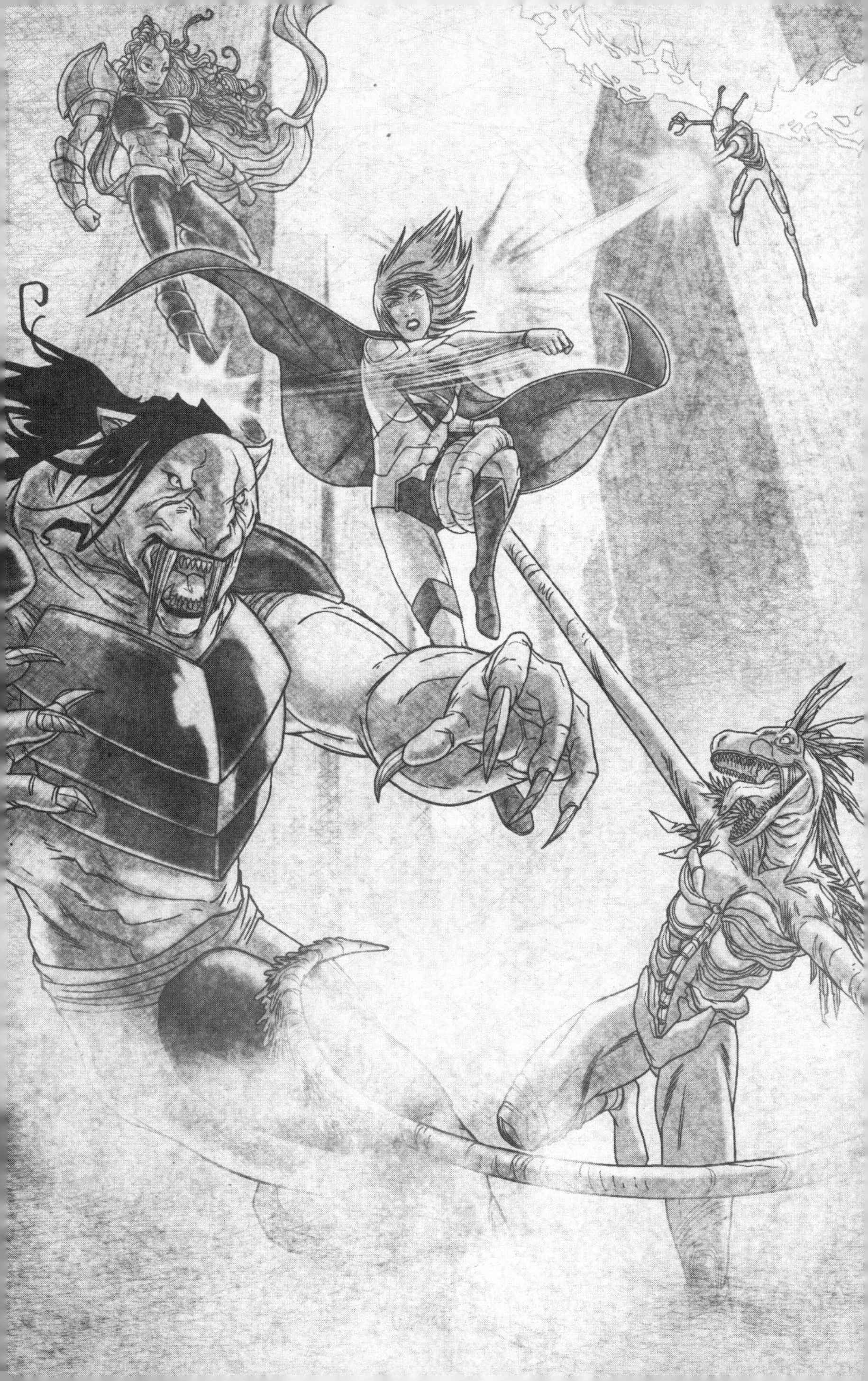

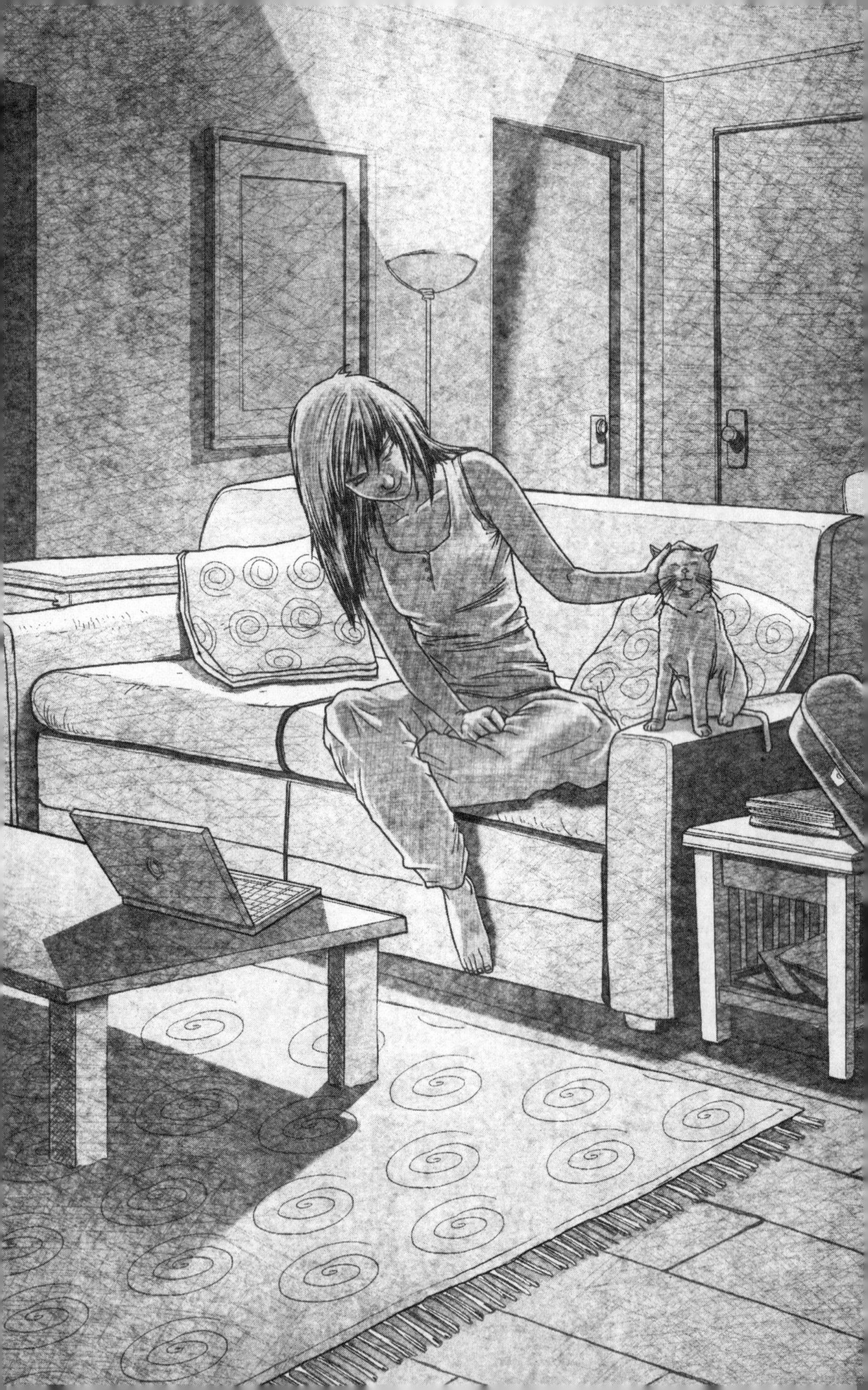

MAKING A HOME

Once Kara revealed herself to the world, it wasn't long before everyone knew about Supergirl. It was up to Kara to make sure that she lived up to their high expectations.

Though protecting the people of Earth was very important to her, she wanted to connect with them, too—to have real friends like she did on Krypton. Making friends was easy on Krypton, where everyone associated with the people in their castes and automatically had something in common.

On Earth, there were no job castes or House connections. Kara didn't know where to start.

Fortunately, she didn't have to make the first move. A young woman named Siobhan Smythe, who had just moved to New York from Ireland, offered to shelter Kara after her battle with the Worldkillers. To Kara's astonishment, Siobhan spoke fluent Kryptonian. Siobhan, who also went by the name Silver Banshee, could instantly speak

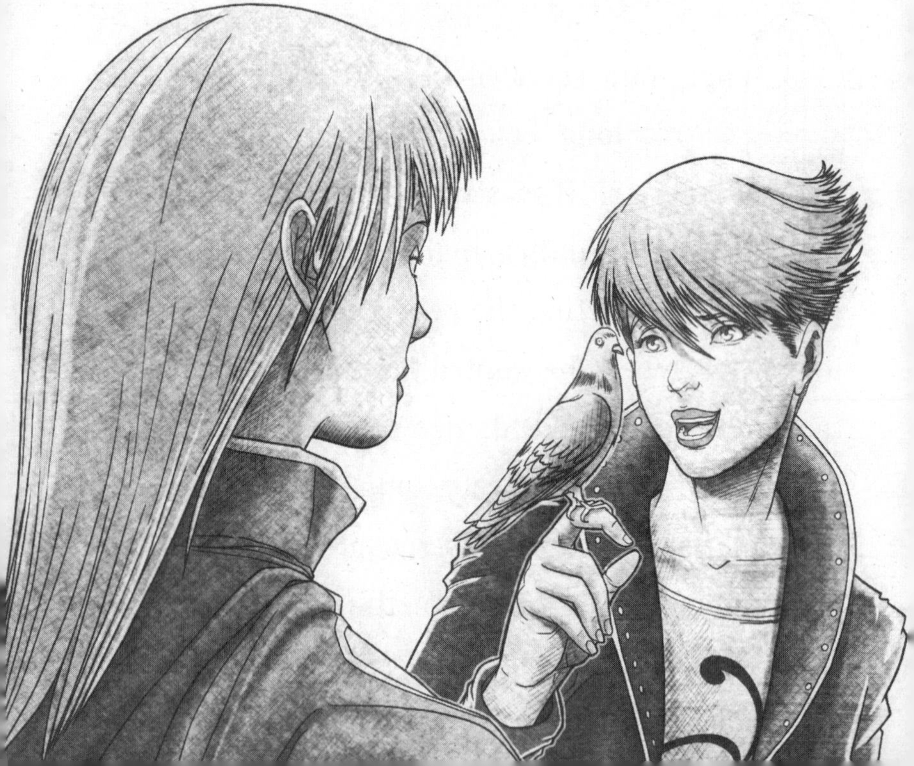

any language perfectly—even animal languages—and had a hypersonic wail that could shatter glass. Earth, Kara realized, was a world of wonders. Her Kryptonian powers weren't as unusual as she had originally thought, not when people like Siobhan had their own amazing abilities rooted in science or magic. Siobhan welcomed Kara into her New York apartment, and the two started a new life as roommates.

Transitioning to everyday life wasn't easy, but with Siobhan's help Kara learned to understand and speak the languages of Earth. Getting used to Earth's strange customs proved a little harder. On Krypton, everything was clean and organized. On Earth, Kara got overwhelmed by the choices on a restaurant menu, and didn't always remember that when you want something from a store, you have to pay for it first. In her free time, Kara enjoyed watching Siobhan perform at music cafés, but had to dial down her super-hearing first so the noisy

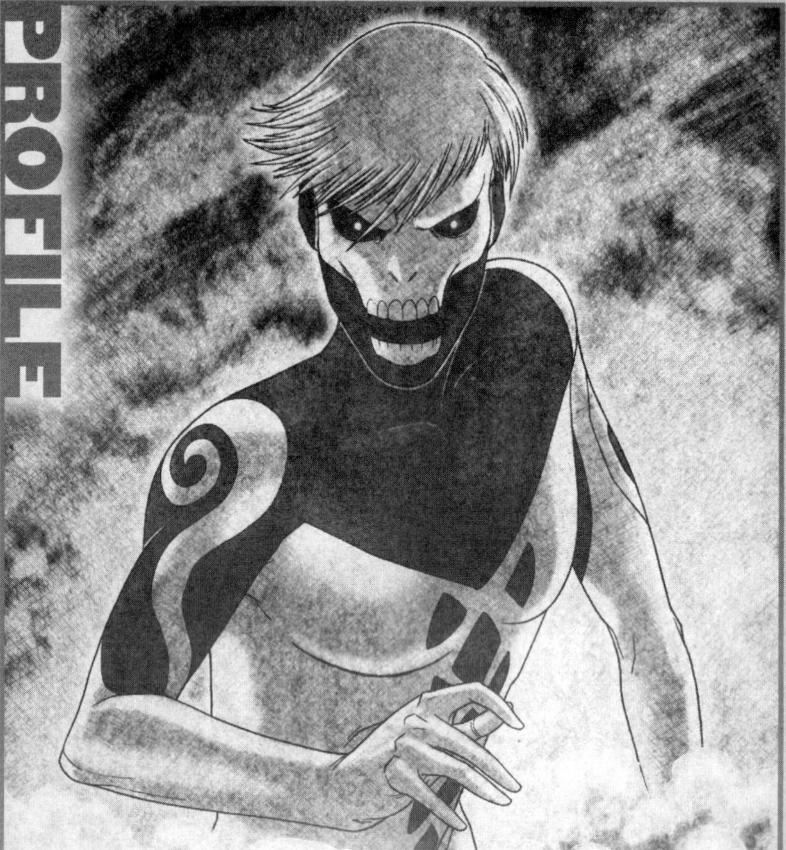
PROFILE

Siobhan Smythe (Silver Banshee)

A magical curse has long haunted the Smythe family of Ireland, causing Siobhan Smythe to possess the bewitching powers of the Silver Banshee. In her normal life, Siobhan is a friendly musician trying to start a new life in New York City.

instruments didn't give her a headache.

Her cousin, Kal-El, had lived his entire life as a native of Earth, which meant that Kara could do the same thing if she wanted. Without her Supergirl costume she looked just like any ordinary human, so she could walk through the streets of New York without anyone recognizing her true identity. With Siobhan's encouragement Kara found a job at a local

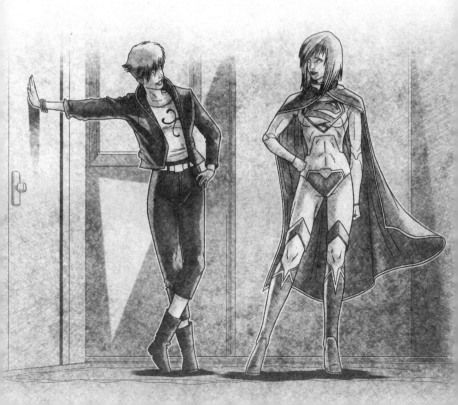

coffee shop. She found the work busy and enjoyable, even if sometimes she forgot her own strength and accidentally pulled the knobs off the espresso machine.

When Kara met Power Girl, it was a shock in many ways. Power Girl came from the parallel dimension called Earth 2, which was similar to

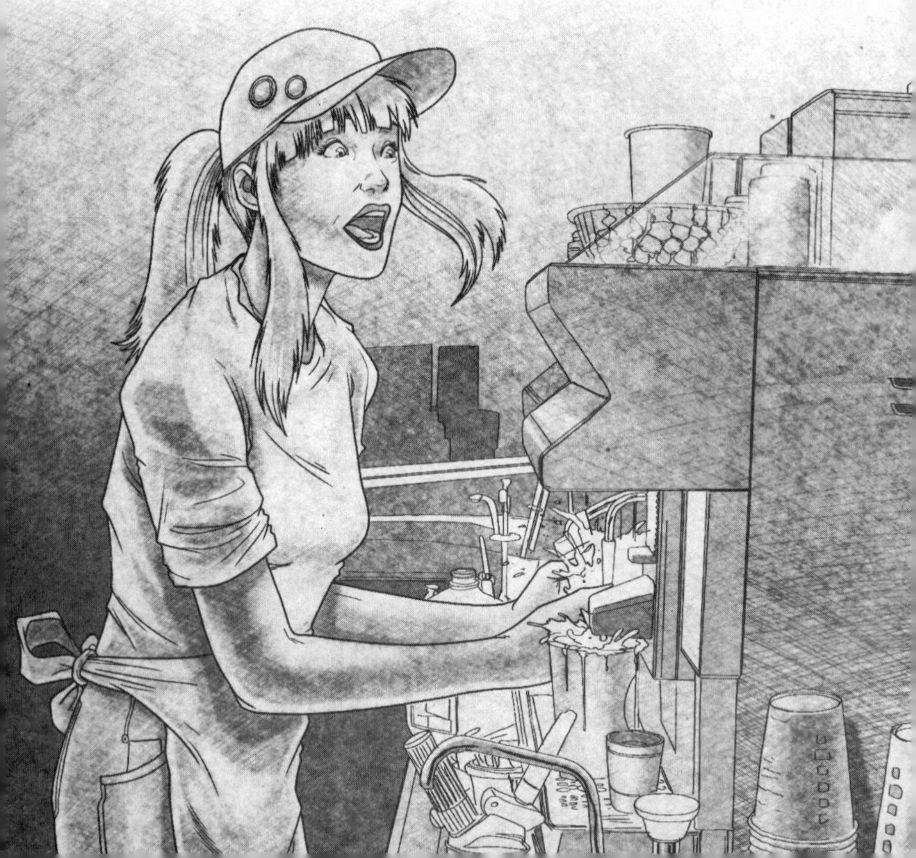

PROFILE

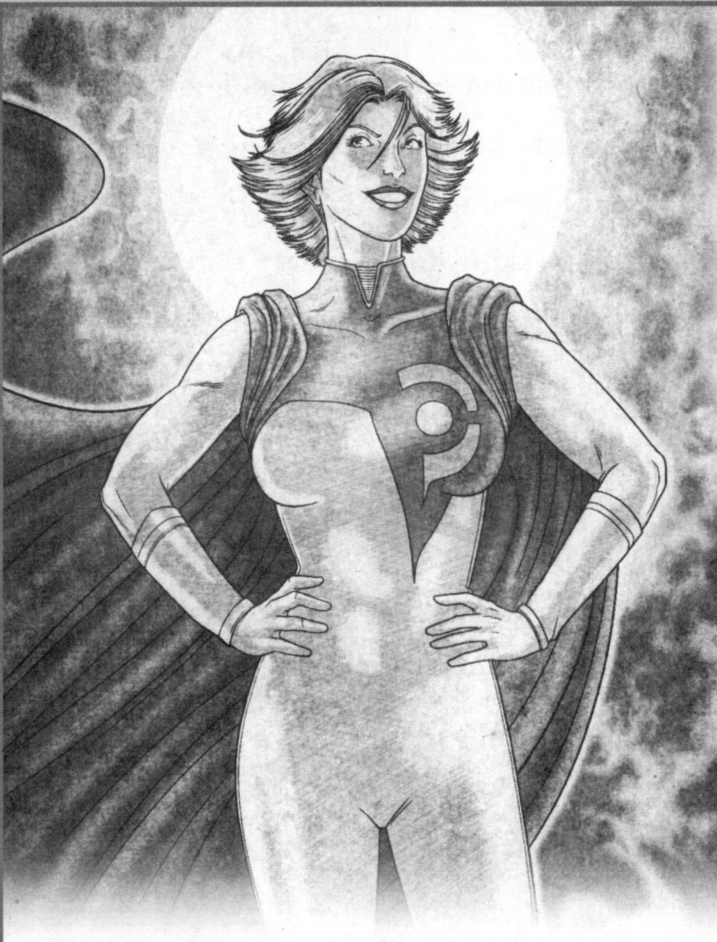

Power Girl

In a parallel universe called Earth 2, history happened differently than it did on the regular Earth. On Earth 2, Kara Zor-El moved on from her Supergirl role to become Power Girl, while also holding down a job as corporate executive Karen Starr. When Power Girl crossed over from Earth 2, she and Supergirl became friends.

Kara's Earth with a few major differences. Power Girl was the Earth 2 version of Kara Zor-El: She was older than Kara and had used her time to become Karen Starr—wealthy CEO of Starr Enterprises—in between her adventures as Power Girl.

At first Kara felt intimidated by Power Girl, believing she could never achieve the same success no matter how long she worked at it. Her counterpart understood what Kara was feeling. Power Girl admitted that she sometimes felt the same way, and that even a business owner and famous hero can still have self-doubts.

Kara realized it was okay if other people—even people who came from a similar background—had faster success or a more glamorous career. It didn't take anything away from her own achievements, and Power Girl's example gave her something new to aim for.

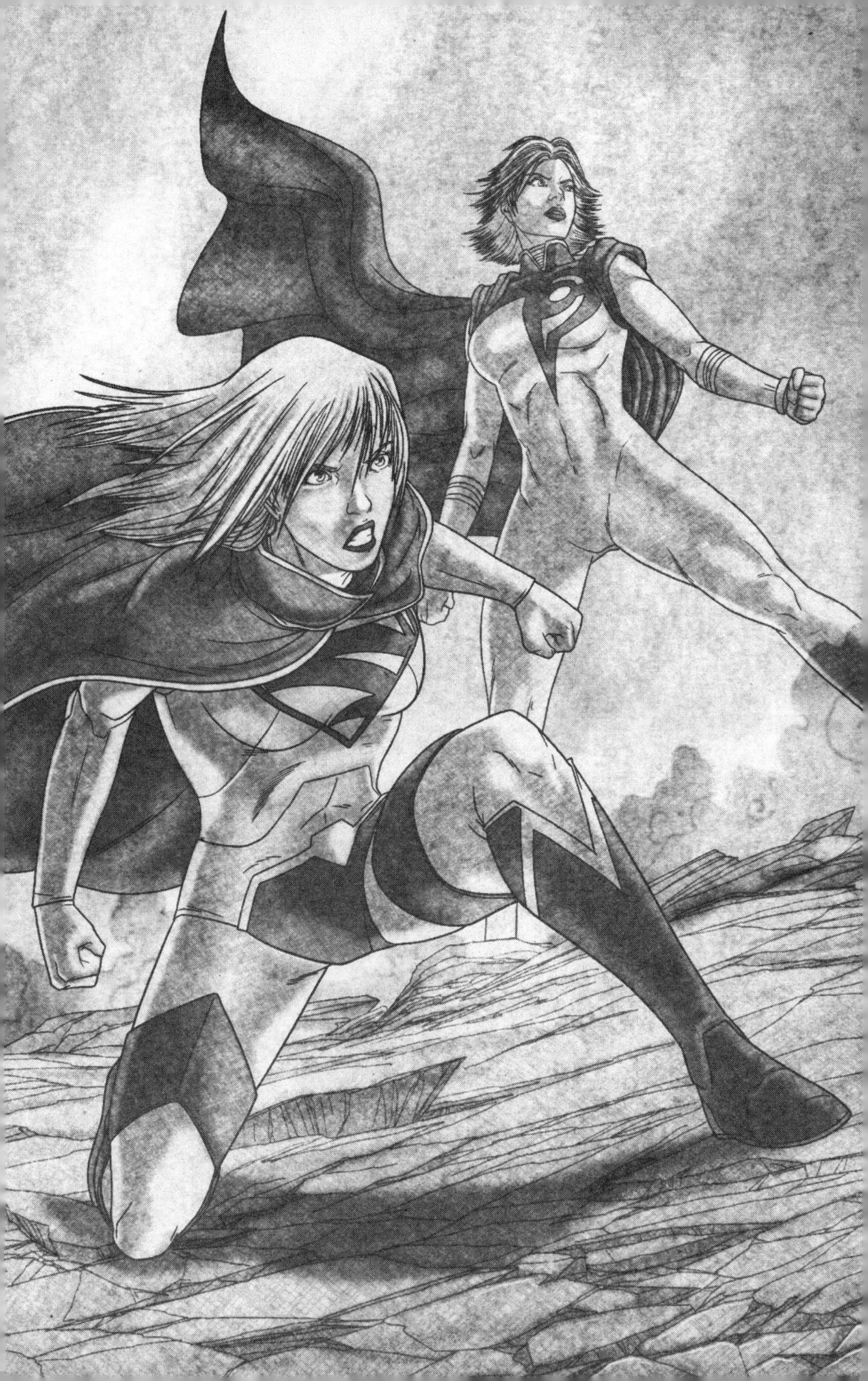

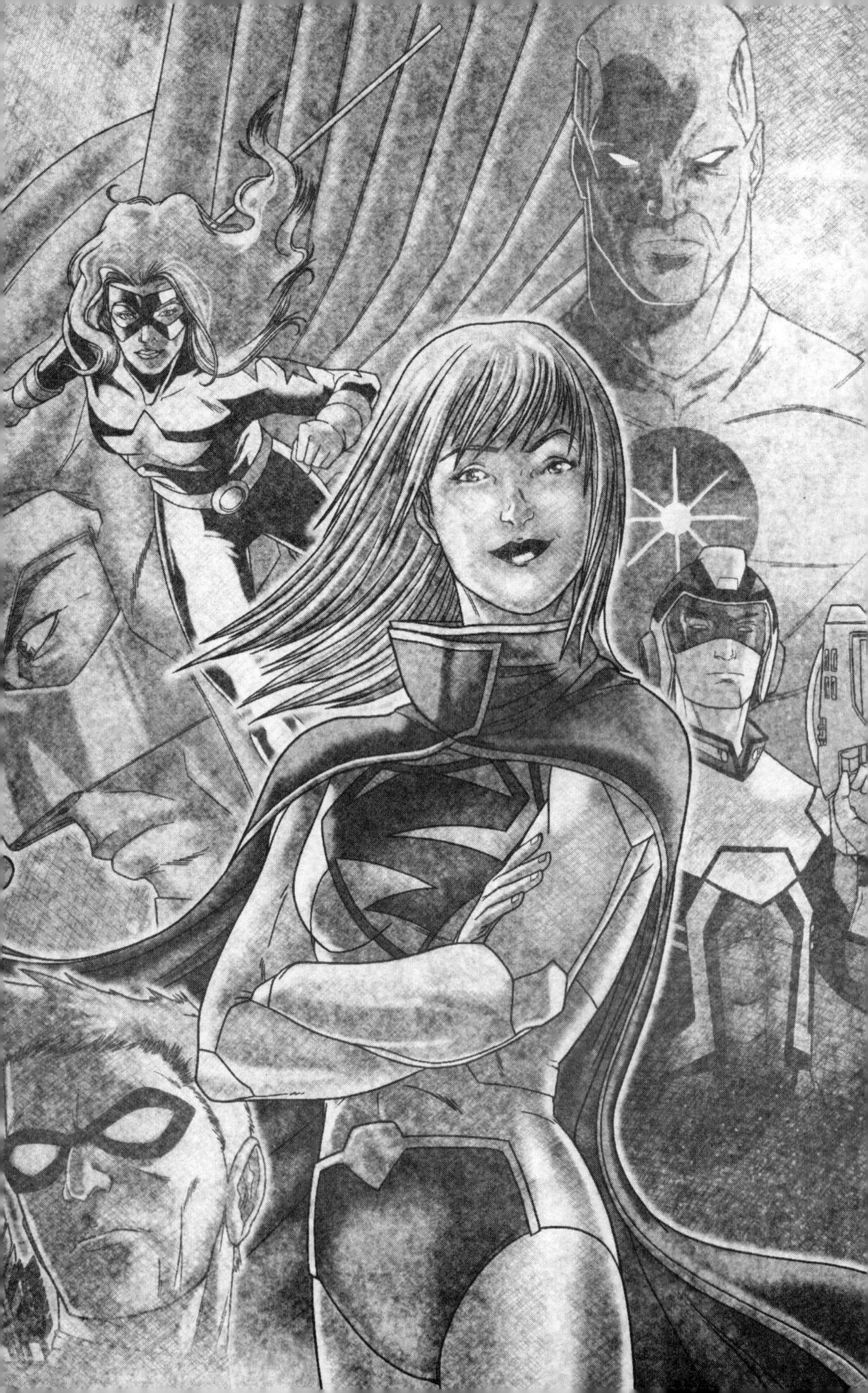

CHAPTER NINE

ALLIES AND ENEMIES

It took time, but Supergirl grew comfortable with her role as a planetary champion. Her cousin Superman had struggled at first as well, and Supergirl discovered that his friends had helped him deal with life as a super-powered alien.

Dr. Shay Veritas was one of those friends, as well as one of the smartest scientists in the world. Kara felt an instant connection with her. Dr. Veritas had been studying Superman's abilities and trying to understand how they were affected by solar radiation, but her most interesting research concerned Kryptonite. This strange mineral, which glowed with green radioactivity, had been formed in the explosion of Krypton and arrived on Earth as meteorites. It was the only substance that could instantly weaken Kara's powers if she came too close to it. Dr. Veritas helped keep Kara safe from the danger of Kryptonite poisoning.

The existence of Kryptonite proved that not everything from Kara's home world was gone forever, so Kara tried to find remains from Krypton that were a little less life threatening. Superman had his own Fortress of Solitude, a Kryptonian structure in the frozen arctic created by a sunstone crystal. When Kara visited, she saw a building that would have looked right at home in Argo City or Kryptonopolis. She even showed Kal-El how to use the control boards, and explained details about Kryptonian culture that he viewed in the Fortress's recordings. It felt good to talk about her former life to someone who was eager to learn more.

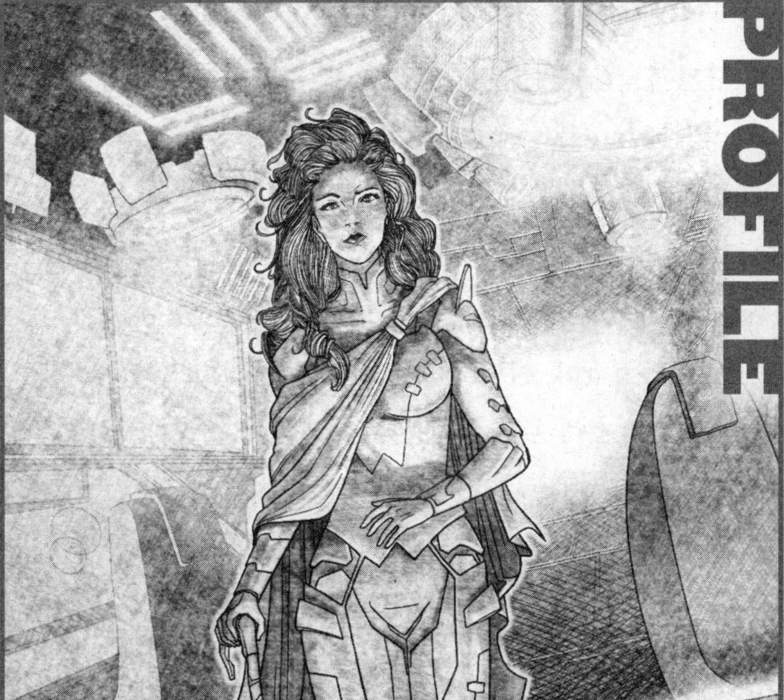
PROFILE

Dr. Shay Veritas

One of the smartest scientists in the world, Dr. Veritas challenges herself by solving problems that are out of this world. She helps Superman and Supergirl understand the limits of their Kryptonian powers using the equipment in the Block, her high-tech research laboratory.

Kara wondered if the same process Kal-El used could create another structure from Krypton, and she soon discovered the answer. When her rocket had arrived on Earth, pieces of its outer shell had burned off and fallen into the ocean. One of those pieces sunk nearly two miles under the waves, all the way to the bottom of the Atlantic. There it had grown into an

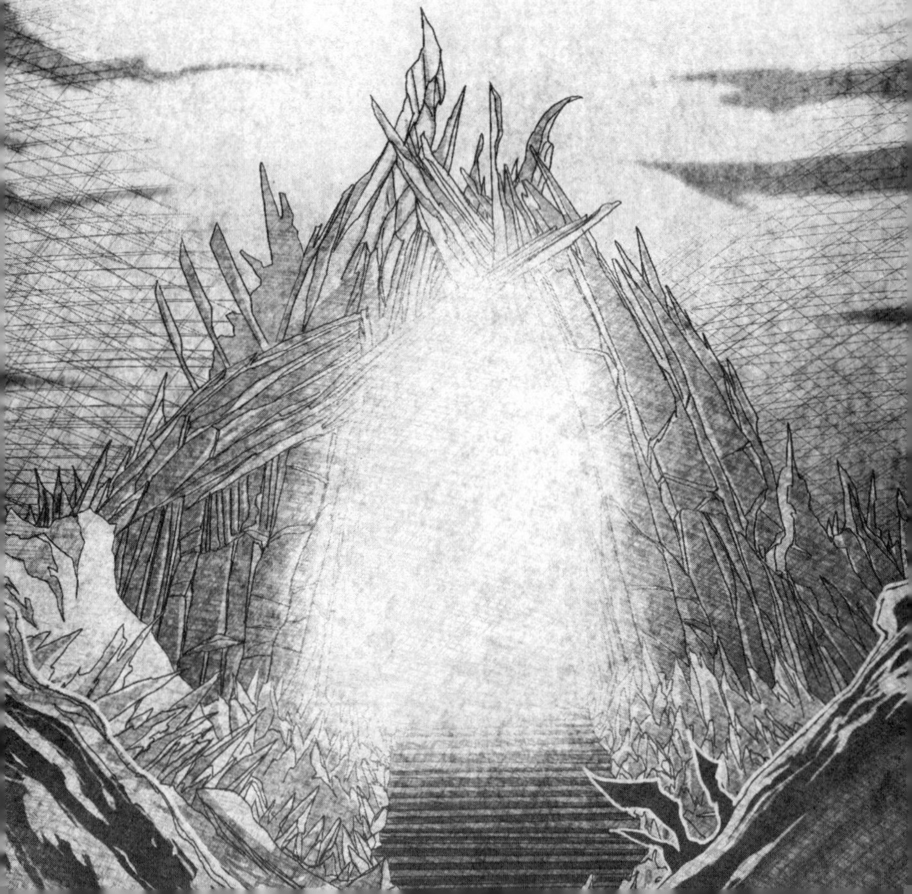

elaborate crystal castle that shone with a pale white light. Only Kara could hold her breath long enough to make the journey to the spot that she named the Sanctuary of Solitude. It was the perfect place to unwind from stress while remembering her favorite things from her former life.

As Kara made more public appearances as Supergirl, she became a target for super-powered enemies. Reign and the Worldkillers were just the beginning. Soon, more foes with ties to Krypton

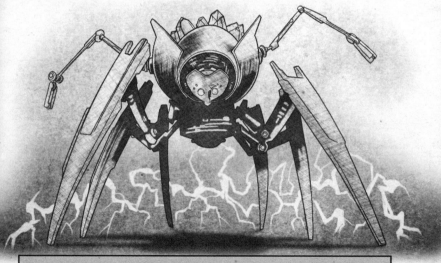

THE SANCTUARY OF SOLITUDE IS PROGRAMMED TO KEEP OUT EVERYONE EXCEPT SUPERGIRL. KRYPTONIAN ROBOTS LIKE THIS ONE ACT AS THE SANCTUARY'S GUARDIANS.

tried to fight Supergirl, including the alien scientist Brainiac, and a half-Kryptonian, half-machine called the Cyborg Superman. When the Cyborg Superman tried to make his body whole again by stealing Kara's body, she defeated him in one of the hardest challenges she had ever faced.

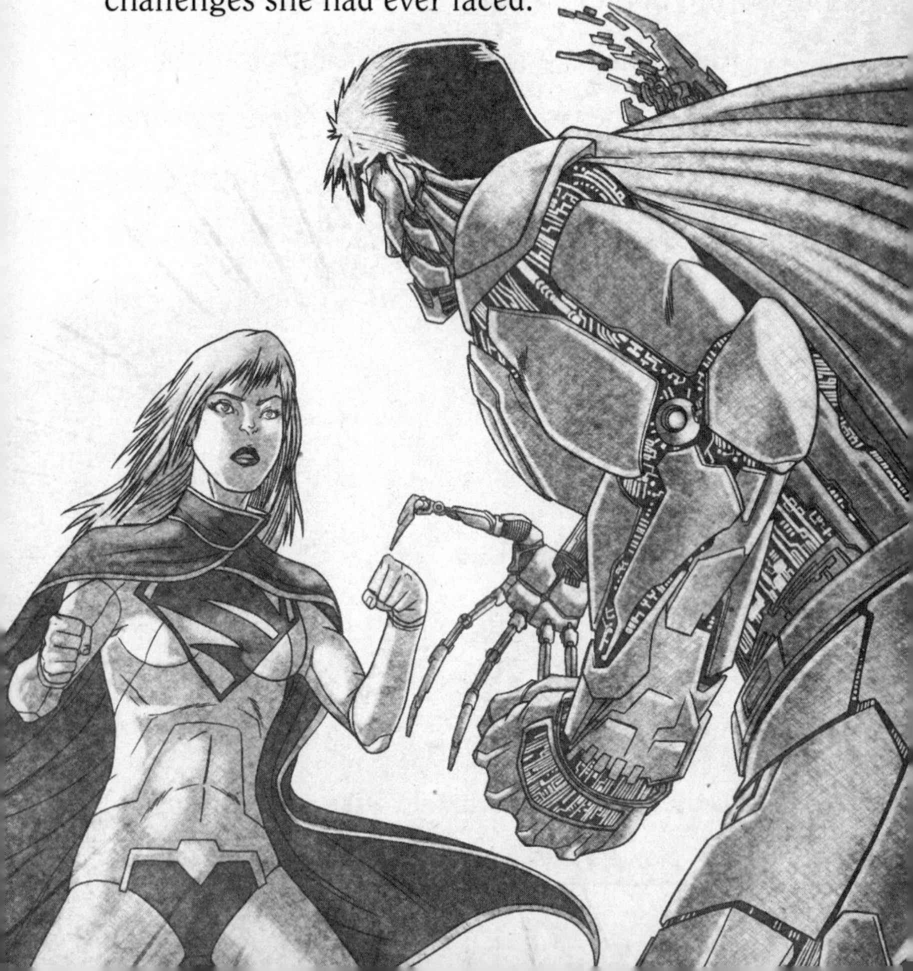

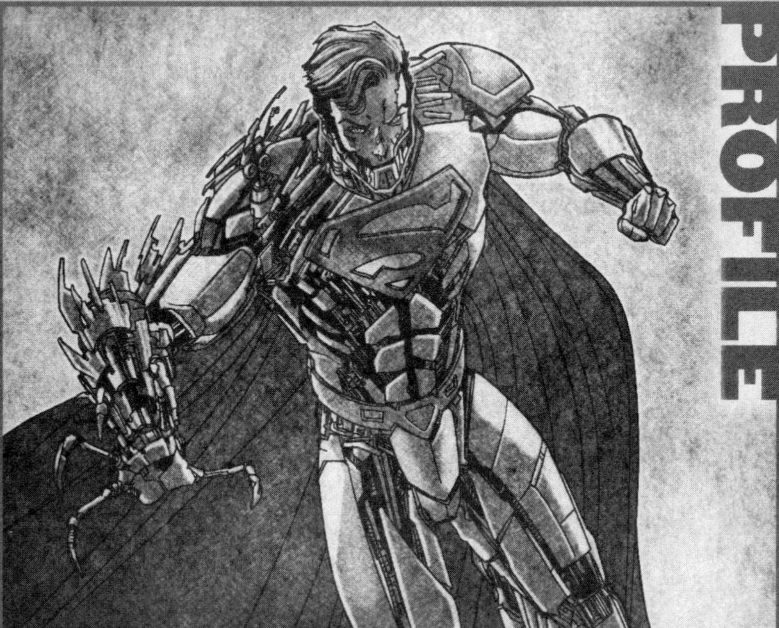
PROFILE

Cyborg Superman

This half-Kryptonian, half-machine creature was created to serve the intergalactic villain Brainiac. He has all the superpowers of a Kryptonian, and can control computer systems using the circuitry in his cybernetic limbs.

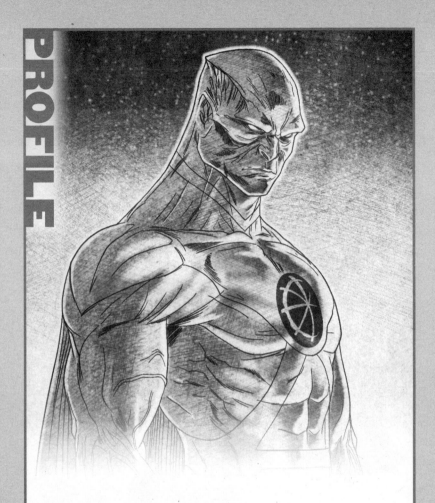

Martian Manhunter

Long ago, a great civilization ruled Mars, but today J'onn J'onzz is the planet's only survivor. Going by the name Martian Manhunter, he became a detective and a Super Hero on his adopted planet of Earth. His powers include shape shifting, flight, and invisibility, but he is weakened by fire.

Luckily, she didn't have to face every threat by herself. Once the other heroes of Earth got to know Supergirl, they invited her to become a member of the team of champions called the Justice League. Supergirl's teammates included Stargirl, an Earth teenager close to Kara's own age, and the Martian Manhunter, who was the last survivor of another alien planet.

The Martian Manhunter told her that when he had suffered from loneliness and loss, he had found fellowship with others. Kara realized that she would never be alone on Earth as long as she worked to stay connected with her new network of friends.

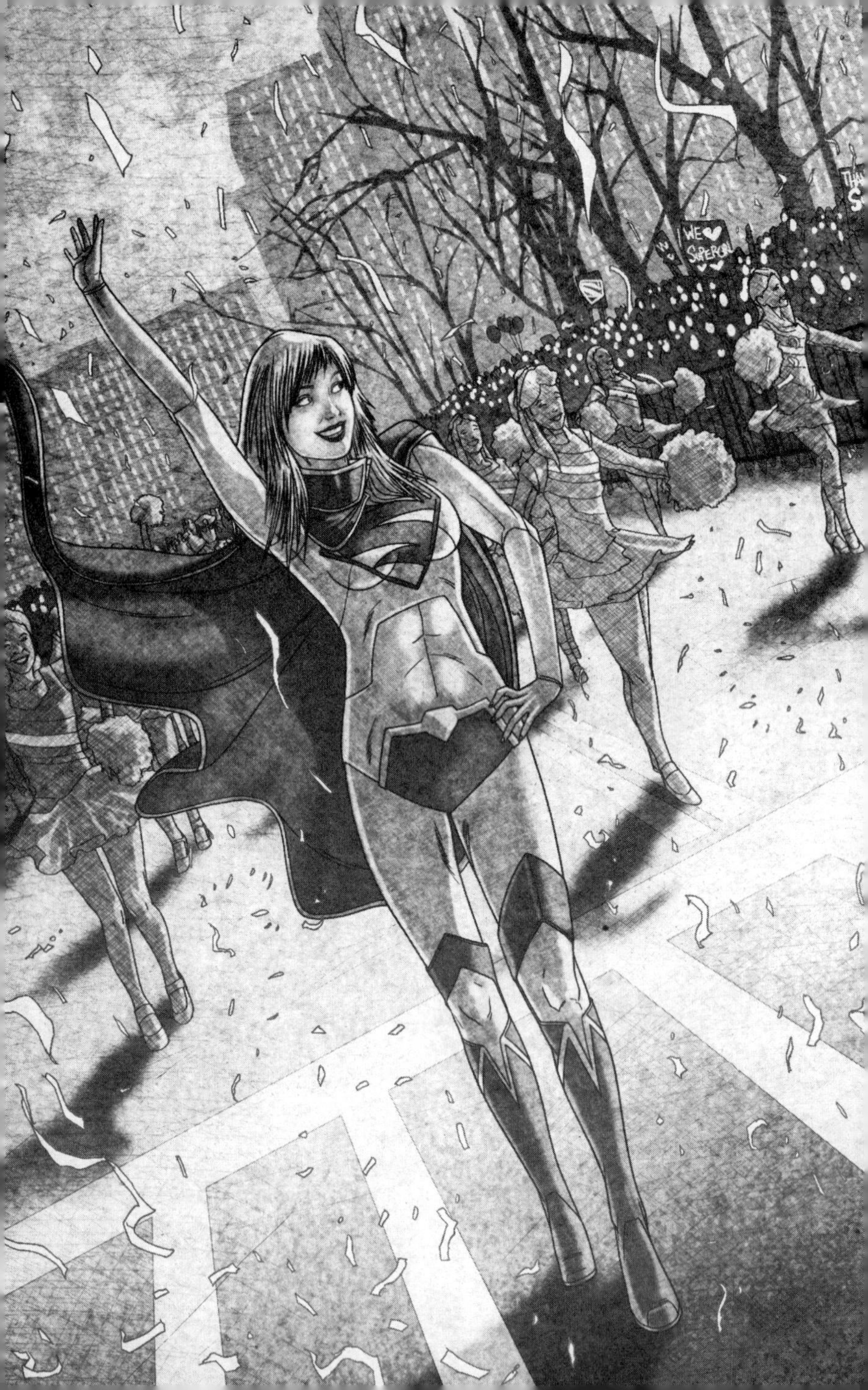
WE ♥

CHAPTER TEN

THE FACE OF HOPE

Since her arrival on Earth, Supergirl has become one of the most beloved Super Heroes in the world. She uses her Kryptonian powers to defend the powerless. She came to this planet as a stranger, but she no longer feels like an outsider.

Supergirl is much more than the famous symbol she wears on her chest. She is powerful and brave, but is also valued for her kind heart and her sharp mind. On Earth, the House of El symbol stands for hope. Through her actions, Supergirl has given

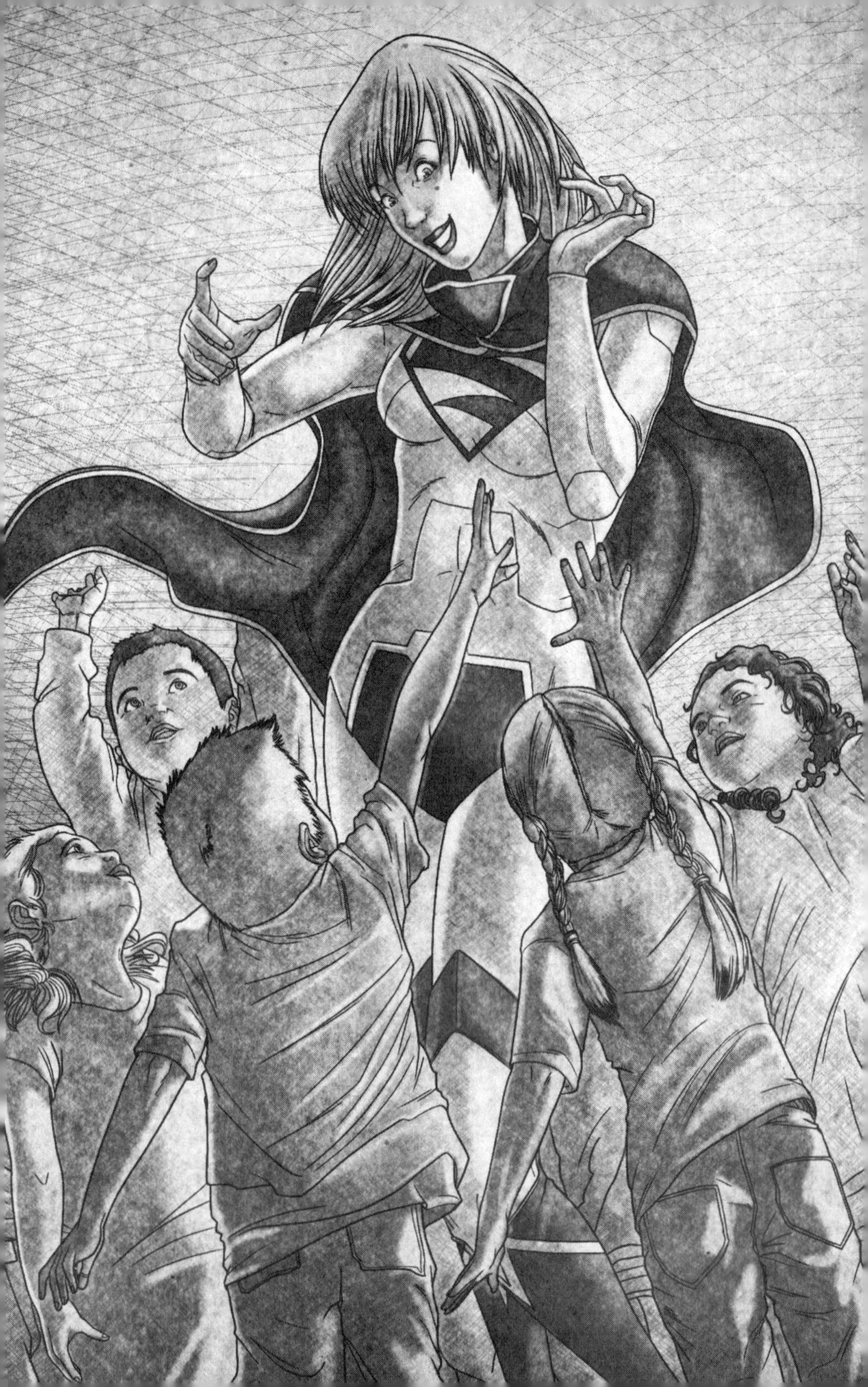

hope to those who need it the most.

People who look up to Supergirl usually see a little of themselves in her. Often they can relate to feeling like an outsider in a strange new place. If Supergirl was able to make a new life after losing everything she knew, others feel confident that they can follow her example.

On Krypton, everyone knew their roles and no one challenged the carefully planned futures that the government had set for them. That's not how it works on Earth at all. This was one of the biggest shocks for Supergirl when she got here, but now it's one of the new ideas she values most. Being athletic and being smart aren't opposites, and Supergirl is glad that she doesn't have to choose one or the other. She is a hero with many strengths.

Supergirl's fight against ignorance and injustice will only continue. She will never give up, and she hopes no one else will, either. The more people that come together to help, the easier it is to win.

The first day that she landed on Earth, Supergirl was confused, terrified, and angry. Today, the people of Earth have accepted her as one of their own—and she is able to truly call this once strange place her new home.

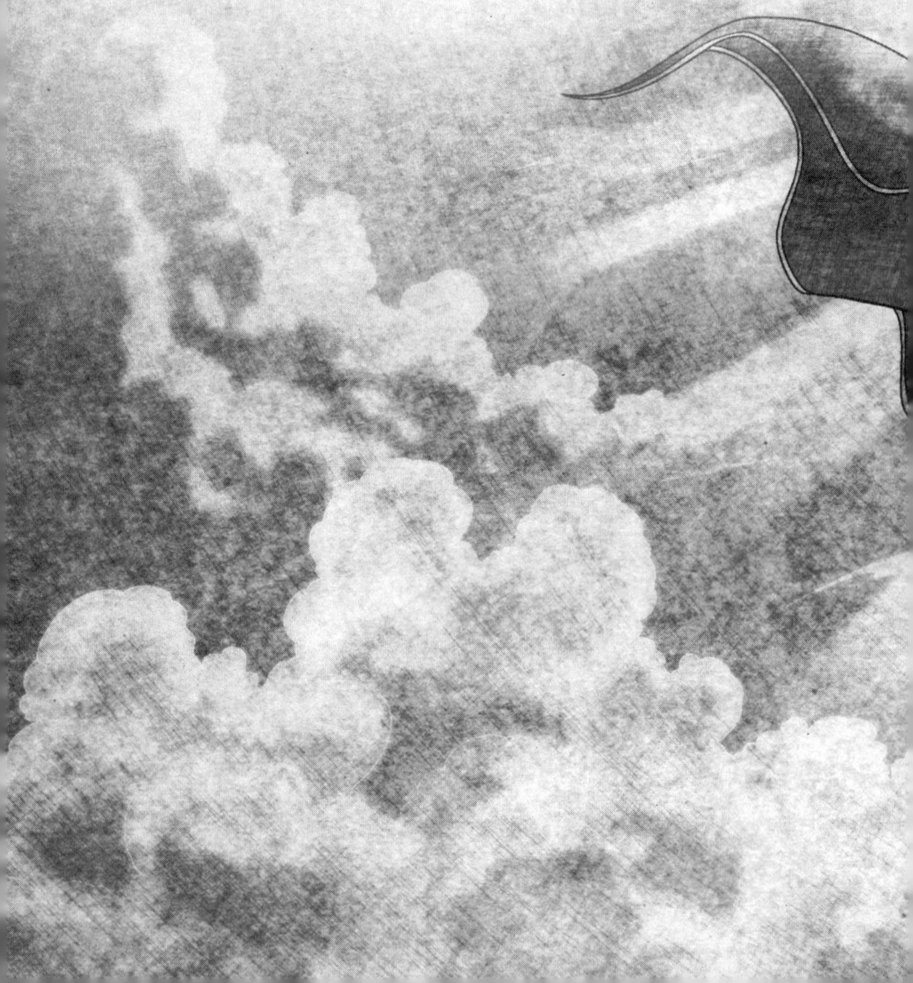

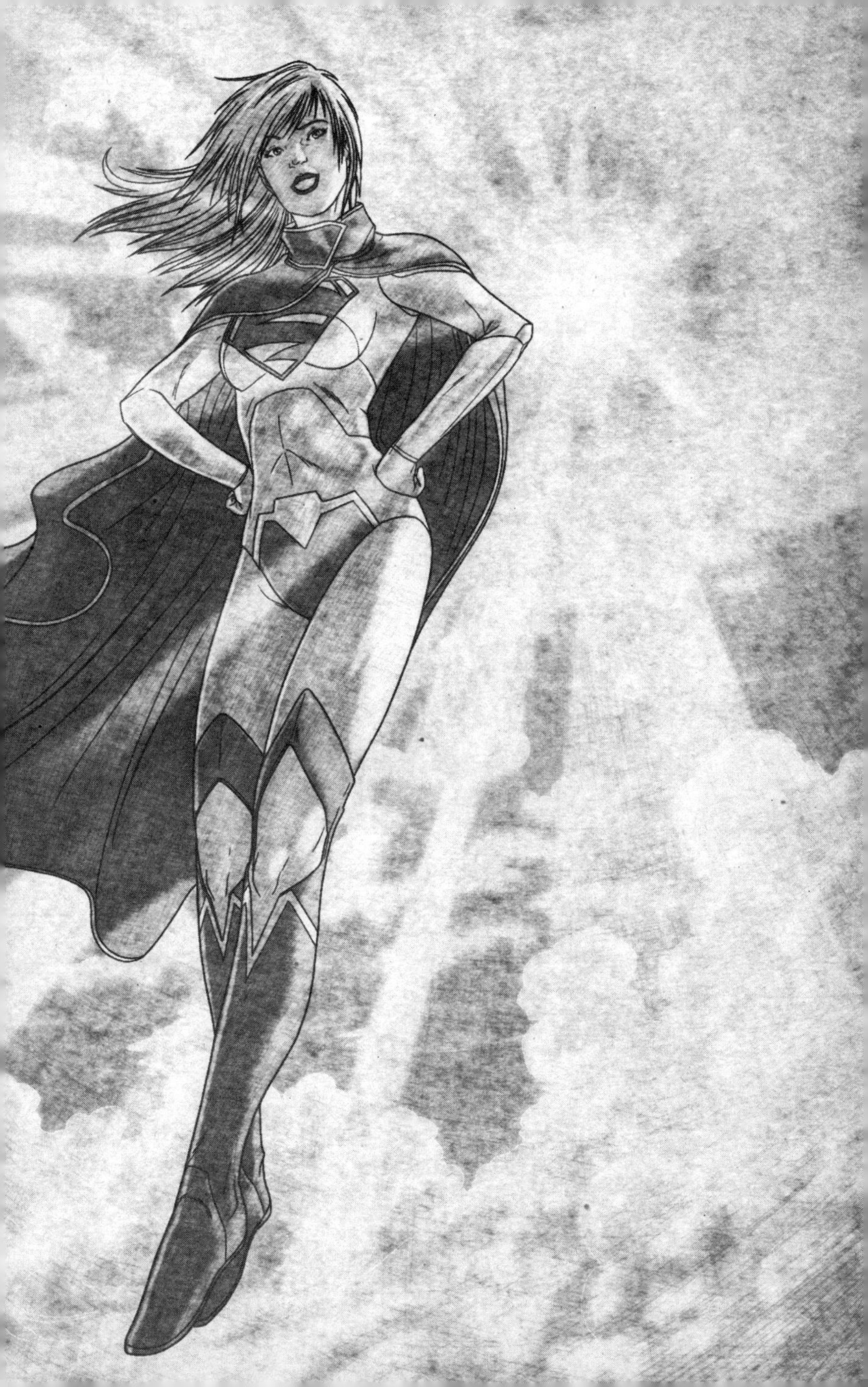

FAST FACTS

✈ Supergirl was born on Krypton and lived there through her teenage years. Like the other members of the House of El, she studied to become a scientist.

✈ Supergirl's father, Zor-El, learned that Krypton would explode. He tried to save their hometown of Argo City with a force field, but his experiment did not work.

✈ Zor-El saved his daughter from Krypton's destruction by sending her to Earth in a rocket. She spent years in suspended animation before she finally woke up.

✈ Superman is Supergirl's cousin. On Krypton, he was called Kal-El.

✈ Kryptonians, like Supergirl, get their powers from the rays of Earth's yellow sun.

◆ Supergirl's powers include flight, super-strength, super-speed, near-invulnerability, X-ray vision, and heat vision.

◆ The costume that Supergirl wears is a formal Kryptonian outfit that symbolizes her status as a member of the House of El.

◆ Supergirl learned English and other Earth languages with the help of her friend Siobhan Smythe, who has the magical ability to understand any language.

◆ In order to better fit in among the people of Earth, Supergirl once worked as a barista in a coffee shop.

◆ Supergirl can hold her breath for hours, and her skin isn't affected by the extremely cold temperatures of outer space.

Because it is made out of Kryptonian material, Supergirl's costume cannot be ripped or damaged.

Unlike Superman, Supergirl is able to raise the temperature of her skin to red-hot levels.

Siobhan Smythe, one of Supergirl's closest friends, is also the magical Silver Banshee. Siobhan's father, the Black Banshee, is her greatest enemy.

Pieces of the planet Krypton have fallen to Earth as Kryptonite, a substance that is harmful to Supergirl.

Supergirl learned how to fight during her self-defense training on Krypton.

Karen Starr, better known as Power Girl, is a different version of Supergirl from another dimension.

The Sanctuary of Solitude at the bottom of the Atlantic Ocean is Supergirl's secret base.

Supergirl is a member of the Justice League with other heroes including Green Arrow, Stargirl, and the Martian Manhunter.

A Kryptonian sunstone stores information and can also create space warps that connect one part of the galaxy with another.

Kryptonian criminals, like General Zod, survived the destruction of Krypton inside a place called the Phantom Zone, and after their escape have become threats to Superman and Supergirl.

Glossary

atmosphere: A mass of gases that surround a planet or star.

caste: A division of society based upon differences of wealth, rank, or job.

chronology: A list of events in order of when they happened.

conquer: To take control of (a country, city, etc.) through the use of force.

crest: A design used to represent a family, group, or organization.

gauntlet: A glove made of small metal plates and worn with a suit of armor.

hologram: A special kind of picture that is made by a laser and looks three-dimensional.

hull: The main body of a large or heavy craft or vehicle (like an airship or tank).

impostor: A person that takes on a false identity or title for the purpose of deception.

insignia: A badge or sign that shows a person is a member of a particular group or has a particular rank.

interstellar: Existing or taking place among the stars.

meteorite: A small body of matter from outer space that makes it to Earth.

orbit: The path taken by one body circling around another body (such as the Earth around the sun).

radiation: Energy (sometimes harmful) that comes from a source in the form of waves or rays you cannot see.

sanctuary: A place that provides safety or protection.

solitude: The quality or state of being alone or away from others.

BACKSTORIES

Uncover the epic histories of your favorite characters!

Read them all!